Windhover

A Journal of
Christian Literature

Volume 6

Windhover: A Journal of Christian Literature

Published at the University of Mary Hardin-Baylor

Publisher:
Jerry G. Bawcom, Ph. D.
President, University of Mary Hardin-Baylor

Editors:
Donna Walker-Nixon
Phyllis Bunnell
Chris Willerton
Joe R. Christopher
Jane Haywood

Editorial Assistant:
Carolyn Poulter

Layout and Design:
Randy Yandell

Vol. VI.

Windhover is published at the University of Mary Hardin-Baylor, Belton, Texas. Subscriptions are $10.00 for one year. Correspondence should be addressed to Donna Walker-Nixon, UMHB Box 8008, 900 College Street, Belton, Texas 76513.

Cover Photo: Grace Episcopal Church in the Plains, Virgina, the second "most photographed" church in Virginia, after the church on the Willamsburg campus of William & Mary.
By: Michael H. Lythgoe

Table of Contents

Jerry Hamby

INSCAPE

I pore over Hopkins' manuscripts,
handwritten drafts of nature sonnets.
As my white-gloved hand turns
the page, I scribble away, copying all
my eyes can absorb. I duplicate insertions,
deletions, inverted lines, musical hooks
denoting counterpoint and sprung rhythm.
I calculate a caesura, the space separating
each half of a line, approximate
the slant of a stress mark.
I see him working at his uncluttered desk,
second-guessing a word choice, scratching
through, then replacing the original,
lamplight fading, ink drying on the page.

The day after he died, another priest
moved about the poet's cloistered cell, feeding
manuscripts to flame. Words popped off the page,
consonants crackling, vowels singing
up the stovepipe. What newly turned nouns
fell through the grate, glowing
among the embers? What conceit danced
about the firebox? What song-silenced bird
soared from the chimney, its inky wings
dissolving in summer smoke?

Angela O'Donnell

HOPKINS IN IRELAND

That is no country for young men,
The fire in whose bones could set aflame
The fields of peat and bogs of cured bodies
That lie beneath the turf of grinning green.

The damp gathers everywhere—in corners, joints and hearts
Suppressing all that leaps to dance and beats to time
And wetting wood and hay and kindling sticks.

To this land you brought the blaze of God's love,
And glowing coals you took from every tongue
To make it catch and light up the world.
Who couldn't guess the smoke and snuff and smolder
Of all that burned within Christ's poet's soul
By the fog and chill, the everlasting rain?

And yet you flamed most bright and brief
In the heart of the desolate dark—
Fire against the ashen sky,
The color of spent embers.

Rhoda Janzen

THE BARGAIN

test

Under the bed's cotton tunnel,
My nightgown's made of flannel,

Bunching damp around my middle.
My sister's much too little

To recognize the need for prayer.
From the darkness on the floor

The lamp's skinny shadow arm
Reaches for my lucky charm.

Now sweating agony I drink the cup
To be beautiful when I'm grown up,

And seal the solemn bargain plea
Like Christ in dark Gethsemane.

testing

At forty-nine, I am a beauty blown,
often forgetting to change the channel
and watching with the volume turned way down.
When my neighbor limbers her soprano
(she boasts that she was twice Miss Illinois),
humiliation rills my eyes with tears.
I cannot explain it. I'm paranoid
since the attack, and now the steps one hears
in hallways seem indifferently evil,
the disembodied of our neighborhoods.
And who would not despair when the dry goods
cocoon, and one honey-colored weevil
becomes a legion, the corn meal moving?
Worms that caress, so little, so loving?

tested

A paid bulimic once in itchy clothes,
I vomited before the fashion shows.

But I find memory in part obscured.
Hair falling out in tufts, nude as a bird

Unnested, plaintively cold, bewitching
blue veins; airsick and violently pitching

Between cities; smoked two reducing packs,
Was photographed with breasts like flaccid sacks.

Solicited, corseted, wind-fanned, taped,
Much sought as wife or mistress as once hoped.

At forty-nine I am a beauty blown.
I have no beauty. I desire none.

Rhoda Janzen

GRAFFITI ANALYST DECLINES HONO-RARIUM

suddenly the fingers of a human hand appeared
and began writing on the plaster of the wall...
                                    —Daniel 5:5

An anthropologist drives a shabby car to South
Central, where he befriends some gangbangers,
graffiti artists. One says, *You wanna see*

graffiti? Man, I'll show you graffiti. On the street
corner he whips off his shirt casually, as if
flicking the lid from a pen. Along his shoulders

Old Roman script bites deep letters into flesh:
SANTA MONICA, a saint revised, a town
displaced. Now in the city's broth of fog

spray paint and jerked syllables writhe out of sense.
Unlike the other documents, these are anonymous.
Yet one summons a stealthy image of young men

at night, swift, severe, tattooed, cleanly operating.
It has nothing to do with sex, though the girls
wait smoking in the car. Pure politics, it is

economy of expression, the broadcast that will bless
the edge of doom. The analyst can read it. He can
tell you what it means—MENE, TEKEL, PARSIN,

unsigned voice of wrath. Letters tight and furled
as new-hatched wings are lighting on the walls,
poised like flies to pulse and reconfigure. And there

will be an angry swarm, lettered and unlettered,
scripted and unscripted, signed and unsigned, saying,
Your days are numbered, readers. Your reign is

at an end. So concludes the analyst, who bows
to the scroll of applause and declines the honorarium
(though the audience is grateful and holds him in esteem.)

Rhoda Janzen

THE RECIDIVIST

Sanka in teeth-indented styrofoam
dignifies the smell of antiseptic
recently applied to vinyl,
powdered methocarbamol,
or omelettes stiff as kindergarten mats.
Now, waking in the blue and starched
and sheeted cubicle, I listen for the nurses
with the a.m. meds, the occupational
therapist with personal grooming tips
(we shave in front of metal mirrors,
thoroughly supervised.) Doctor's mouth,

masked sunny tangerine, kisses law: "You need"—
crossing and uncrossing legs with an earnestness
I richly appreciate—"stress management."
(Mismanagement devolves from trazodone;
one's grave intentions are misconstrued.)
Ray likes to smear the walls with excrement,
a signature which exacts the promise of
an untranslated testament. Dull as gnats,
the orderlies write off Ray's hieroglyphs,
coded prophecies that the team of Daniels
never cracks. We who are suicidally depressed,

or, as the well-groomed doctor says,
unmanageably stressed, admire
the breviary. The recidivist bows
over the Sanka and passes the cup
to imaginary supplicants, lost tribes of Israel.
The nurses brook no arguments. Shambling
down the hall, shoes naked and unlaced,
tongues displaced as in a long-awaited Pentecost,
we nod to the mighty Yahweh who pried Israel
out of Egypt at a not unreasonable price.
We are the sons of Levi, patient for our Christ.

Rhoda Janzen

ZERO HOUR

Whiskery arms akimbo, seniors gamely
plunge into the beat, or try to. Water aerobics:
zero hour where time doesn't swim as it does
Stateside—it lounges by the pool, hammocked,
sighing ineluctably. We wooly mammoths
have strayed in tar. Rodolpho bends over us,
his shirt's hundred peacock eyes winking:
Beautiful ladies first, why not ? Somebody reads
the cards we send to Los Angeles, where every
hour reverses zero. It's all reversal here:
bodies shuck their husks like great pale Jonahs
fled from Nineveh. Clouds chop the sky,
ominous as a testament. We roll over, we burn.
Even with the lazy rain, we'll never leave
the pool's rim—except when zero counts to one.
We sign a tip for coconut, and we are spent.
God's up there, rumbling, a tropical front.

                    I

Nut-brown, dry as philopenas, we pay
the tardy bills. The handsome stray pricks
the screen, jingling. His new collar indicates
he loves somebody else; he's moving on. Low
on the linoleum, his jaws crack dry catfood,
as if to say each hour after zero marches uniform.
The cat's tiny clenched anus dots the exclamation.
This hindnote of surprise or suddenness is the last
I see of him. Yet why should we be surprised,
since on the clock zero can't begin to count
without its one? Why, when they threw him
overboard and the raging sea grew calm?

Hugh Cook

AN OVERCOAT OF CLAY

Her gravestone, a modest white rectangular slab bevelled at the edges, stands behind a waist-high railing of ornamental black iron in Amherst's West Cemetery. To the left and of equal height stands the gravestone of her sister Lavinia; to the right and a foot taller, that of her father and mother. Her gravestone is inscribed with the following words:

EMILY DICKINSON
BORN
DEC. 10, 1830
CALLED BACK
MAY 15, 1886

Resting precariously on top of the gravestone this June day lie two white daisies, still fresh, their stems wrapped with a curl of turquoise ribbon. At the foot of the gravestone, in grass worn bare by the feet of visitors, lie five or six copper pennies.

On a recent trip to the east coast during which we visited a number of New England literary shrines, my wife Judy and I included a stay in the town of Amherst, Emily Dickinson's life-long home. We visited the Dickinson gravesite and toured the Homestead, where Dickinson spent all but fifteen years of her life, and within which she became a recluse the last twenty-five years of her life. Standing inside Emily Dickinson's bedroom, I was struck by the surprising shortness of the bed, and thought of her poem which begins, "Ample make this Bed—/ Make this Bed with Awe—."

In 1840 when Emily was 10, the Dickinson family moved from the Homestead on Main Street to a white frame house a mile away on North Pleasant Street, from which Dickinson had a view of the West Cemetery, and so was able to observe the burial of Amherst citizens. In fact, five of her school friends died of consumption and were buried in the West Cemetery during her stay on North Pleasant Street.

In a letter dated January 12, 1846, Dickinson said to her school friend Abiah Root, "I have just seen a funeral procession go by. . .so if my ideas are rather dark you need not marvel." Nor need any reader of Dickinson's poetry marvel, for it is immediately apparent that from her youth to her death in 1886 Dickinson had a life-long obsession with human mortality, which she referred to as "an Overcoat of Clay." Death, the "sweet Darkness," the "supple Suitor" "who drills his Welcome in—," was a subject to which Dickinson "returned more frequently than to any other," says biographer George Frisbie Whicher. "There are poems of Dickinson," states Albert J. Gelpi, ". . . whose necrophilic preoccupation outdoes everybody except perhaps Poe."

The source of Dickinson's "anguish" (one of the more often recurring words in her poetry) concerning death was twofold. The first agony was her own uncertainty concerning what lay beyond the grave. In one poem (#501), Dickinson demonstrates the ambivalence that characterizes so much of her writing. The poem's first lines ring with faith and affirmation:

> This World is not Conclusion.
> A species stands beyond—
> Invisible, as Music—
> But positive, as Sound—

Soon, however, the poem struggles to solve the riddle which "beckons" and "baffles," namely whether or not there is life after death. Expressing her vexed uncertainty on this question, Dickinson closes the poem with a striking metaphor: "Narcotics cannot still the Tooth—/ That nibbles at the soul—." A letter to her cousins Louisa and Fannie Norcross written immediately after the death of Dickinson's mother expresses similar uncertainty. "Like a flake gathered by the wind she is now part of the drift called Infinity," Dickinson wrote of her mother. "We don't know where she is, though so many tell us." And in a letter to Charles H. Clark dated June 16, 1883 after the death of Clark's brother James, Dickinson wrote, "Are you certain there is another life? When overwhelmed to know, I fear that few are sure."

In July of 1884, after the death of Dickinson's eight-year-old nephew Gilbert of typhoid fever, Dickinson wrote to Fannie and Louise Norcross,

> The going from a world we know
> To one a wonder still
> Is like the child's adversity
> Whose vista is a hill,
> Behind the hill is sorcery
> And everything unknown,
> But will the secret compensate
> For climbing it alone?

"Will the secret compensate/ For climbing it alone?"—this was a question, as Roger Lundin points out in his illuminating biography of Dickinson, that haunted the poet the last years of her life.

The second agony for Dickinson was the anguish of separation from a loved one, which Dickinson spoke of as "All we know of heaven,/ And all we need of hell," a pain so severe it leaves "Kindred as responsive/ as Porcelain." Poem after poem and letter after letter record Dickinson's anguish over the loss of friends and loved ones now "sleeping the churchyard sleep." It would be well for us to keep in mind the reality of the nineteenth-century experience of death which, as Lundin reminds us, did not often occur in the distant sterility of a hospital, but invaded the intimacy of the home. It was the custom for family members to keep vigil at the bedside of an ill or dying person, and Dickinson had kept such vigil on numerous occasions, including a watch of two nights during the dying of Sophia Holland, which Dickinson afterward spoke of as "the two most terrifying nights of her life," and the aforementioned death of her mother, of which Dickinson later said in a letter, "Blow has followed blow, till the wondering terror of the Mind clutches what is left, helpless of an accent—."

It is not often in our day of sterile hospitals that one experiences another person's dying so immediately as Dickinson did, yet only recently, and within a space of six months, I stood at the deathbeds of two women whose dying I was privileged to witness. I say "privileged" for, despite the anguish accompanying both deaths, they were also sacred moments of appalling beauty. It was this paradox of death's anguish and sacredness that drove me to read Dickinson again, and her thoughts concerning this duality run through this essay as a means to help me explore the import of the two deaths I recently experienced. The women's names are Ann Kloet and Alice DeKleine. Let me tell you their story.

***

The town of Ancaster, population 25,000 and growing, lies on the western edge of the city of Hamilton, Ontario. It is a town that is proud of its core, a picturesque street of churches, stores, and homes known as "the village." There is an old-world quality to the village that is created by a number of Niagara escarpment limestone buildings: St. John's Anglican Church, the township hall, office buildings, stores, and homes. Even the Tim Horton's donut shop—normally a prototype of fast-food architecture—here, in the village, is built of faux limestone.

Adrian Kloet owns the Shell gas station in the village; he's been at this location twenty years. He and Ann met back in the 1950s shortly after both their families had immigrated from the Netherlands and become part of the Dutch Reformed community in Hamilton. Adrian courted Ann and they married in Mount Hamilton Christian Reformed Church in 1964. They raised cucumbers for a while on a hobby farm near Simcoe, then Adrian bought a gas station in Hamilton. Ann never worked outside the home, choosing instead to be a full-time mother to the four children that were born to them. She enjoyed gardening and going for walks in the beautiful wooded property within view of the escarpment she and Adrian moved to eight years ago.

But life in their idyllic retreat was not perfect. Ann had gradually begun to develop an alcohol dependency, drinking vodka, as many alcoholics will. Probably the most significant event in Ann and Adrian's married life was Ann's decision in 1991 to own up to her addiction. It was not an easy decision: after years of denial, she finally called the church's Family Outreach program and admitted her alcoholism. "That was one of the best days of our life," Adrian says. I was there the day Ann shared the news during the time for prayer requests at our church, Fellowship Christian Reformed, and the church rallied to her support. The congregation made the decision to switch from wine to grape juice at holy Communion. Ann and Adrian attended weekly A.A. meetings. I would be hesitant to tell you these things about Ann if she herself had not been so open about her addiction, if she had not stood up every week at public meetings and said, "My name is Ann, and I am an alcoholic."

Adrian says now that her bout with alcoholism changed Ann: "She began to open up," he says, "and became more caring. Not that she wasn't before," he adds quickly, "but . . . ." He pauses. "You begin to realize what's important in life and what isn't."

Five years after conquering her alcohol addiction, however, Ann would face a far greater battle. In the fall of 1996 she began to feel discomfort in her abdomen, which had begun to enlarge. Ann visited her doctor and, after tests were conducted at Thanksgiving, a diagnosis was made: ovarian cancer. Shortly thereafter Ann shared this news too during prayer time at Fellowship Church. I recall the sense of shock falling on the congregation as Ann stood and broke the news. After the service, someone requested that members of the congregation stay for a special time of prayer. About fifty people stood in a circle and prayed fervently for Ann's healing.

Chemotherapy began, and Ann lost her hair. After the first round was over, Ann was tested. "The minute the doctor walked through the door," Adrian says, "I could see on his face . . . ." He does not finish the sentence. Several more rounds of chemo followed. The family remained hopeful. Fellowship Church prayed for her continuously. After her latest treatment Ann's hair began to grow back, so that she looked even stylish with her short grey hair.

The cancer, however, persisted. A year later it had reached a critical stage.

***

Alice DeKleine immigrated to Brockville, Ontario with her family in 1952, the prototypical Dutch immigrant family of ten children. Alice was 14. A year later Dick, himself a recent Dutch immigrant, came calling. He and Alice "went together" for six years before they married in Brockville in 1959. Alice had begun work at a pharmaceutical company; Dick was a foreman at Black & Decker, the manufacturer of electrical hand tools. When the company experienced rapid growth, adding an extra shift, then another, the stress began to take its toll on Dick, and he began to explore his dream of starting his own business. He had studied architecture and was skilled in woodworking; he decided, with a partner, to begin a cabinet-making business. When he contacted Manpower Canada as to what would be a promising location for such a business he was told Hamilton was the place to go. Dick and Alice moved to the Steel City.

Five children would be born to them; like Ann, Alice decided to stay home with her growing family. It seemed their own children weren't enough, however, for Dick and Alice developed a love for "fostering," and over the years have been foster parents to 35 children. This gift of caring for others always characterized Alice DeKleine; friends will mention that Alice always brought meals to families in need and sent cards to the sick. She was also a pioneer: she began a Ladies Auxiliary in her church; she founded the Friendship Club, a program for the developmentally disabled, at Fellowship Church; she was the first woman deacon elected in the Niagara region of the Christian Reformed Church. As an elder serving on Council with Alice, I experienced firsthand Alice's compassion and care for others; she was an excellent deacon, always looking for opportunities to serve others.

Thursday afternoon, December 3, Alice was alone in the house with Alycia, their fifteen-year-old foster child. Dick had gone to a craft show in Toronto with their daughter Carolyn, exhibiting the iron and stone sculpture Carolyn's husband Floyd makes. Alice was preparing the house for Christmas, hanging cedar wreaths and garlands on the walls with Alycia. Suddenly she began to experience a severe headache, complaining of the sound of a rushing wind in her ears. She lay down on the couch and asked Alycia to soak a cloth in cold water to place on her forehead. Then she must have had a sense that things were more serious, for she asked Alycia to run next door. A neighbour came, and called 911. The ambulance arrived and took Alice to McMaster University Medical Centre.

At 5:20 that afternoon Dick received a telephone call at the craft show in Toronto from his son Brian. Carolyn thought it was news that her sister Debbie, who was expecting her first child at any time, had had her baby in Oshawa. Instead, Dick had to tell Carolyn that her mother had been rushed to the hospital with what appeared to be a brain aneurism, and that things did not look good. Medical staff were experiencing difficulty stabilizing Alice, therefore it was not until six hours later that she was transferred to Hamilton General Hospital, a trauma centre, where she was placed in the Intensive Care Unit. She was in a coma. Nevertheless the family had reason, at first, to be hopeful. Alice responded to Dick's presence in the room by twitching a finger or making some other body movement whenever Dick spoke to her, but her blood pressure would also rise to a dangerous level. Doctors informed Dick that, difficult though it was, he would have to limit his visits and not speak as often to Alice.

**

After her cancer reached the critical stage, Ann and Adrian made the decision that Ann would not go to a hospital, but would stay—and die, it now appeared—at home. A hospital bed was set up for Ann in the dining room of their house directly in front of two bay windows, one facing east, the other south. From the windows Ann was able to enjoy a panoramic view of the Kloets' yard: a white balustered porch railing three feet away, a white bird feeder in the east window, then a riot of green—walnut trees, shrubs, evergreens, lawn. The grass slopes steeply away from the house towards a curved gravel driveway; beside the driveway lies a pond, its sides lined with stones. In the distance, only a mile away, the horizon consists of a smoky green line of trees at the top of the Niagara escarpment. From the bay window facing east and through all the foliage, you can see the semitrailer trucks, as small as Dinky toys, inch their way up Highway 403 climbing the escarpment.

By now, Ann's cancer was in an advanced stage, and the chemotherapy was stopped. Despite that, she and Adrian managed to go for short walks together. When the pain that came with eating became too excruciating, Ann stopped taking food altogether. Mornings, Adrian says, were particularly painful for Ann, and she would hold her head in her hands. Adrian bought a burial plot in Good Shepherd Garden of White Chapel cemetery.

As an elder at Fellowship Church I asked Adrian whether Ann might wish to have holy Communion at home, a ritual performed only in extreme instances. Several days later Adrian informed Peter, our pastor, that Ann would like to do so, that she and Adrian had in fact talked about the possibility. We set a date when Peter and I would come: 11:00 a.m., Friday, May 29.

That Friday morning was sunny and warm. Peter picked me up at 10:45 in the new minivan he and his wife Grace had just bought. We drove silently, aware of the gravity of our visit. Peter and I had often administered to each other the bread and juice of Communion in church, but never to anyone dying at home. I had not seen Ann for several months, and was apprehensive about what I would see. Peter's minivan climbed the Kloets' curving driveway.

Adrian met us at the door. We stepped into the house; in the dining room to our right, Ann lay on the bed, its one end raised. When I saw Ann, my heart groaned—with her emaciated body, gaunt face and bald scalp, she looked like an inmate of a Nazi concentration camp.

Peter went to prepare the Communion elements in the kitchen and returned moments later with a plate holding pieces of bread and a glass of juice. The room was filled with bright sunlight streaming through the windows. I noticed a photo of Ann when she was healthy hanging on the wall between the bay windows. We sat around Ann's bed, Adrian at Ann's feet, Peter and I at her side, and spoke with Ann of the promise of spring, of God's faithfulness with the seasons. I wondered whether this was a difficult topic of conversation for Ann, wondered whether a person about to die would want to talk about the beauty of the earth. Ann seemed very subdued. I thought of Emily Dickinson's description of the weighty stillness in the room of one dying as being like "the Stillness in the Air—/ Between the Heaves of Storm—." As I sat right beside Ann, I saw now that her hair had actually begun to grow again, a soft down visible on her scalp beneath a few longer hairs.

The room became quiet, and Peter said we would celebrate Communion. He began to read: "Come to me, all you who are weary and burdened, and I will give you rest. Take my yoke upon you and learn from me, for I am gentle and humble in heart, and you will find rest for your souls." Then he spoke the Words of Institution: "The Lord Jesus, on the night he was betrayed, took bread, and when he had given thanks, he broke it and said, 'This is my body, which is for you; do this in remembrance of me.' In the same way, he took the cup, after supper, saying, 'This cup is the new covenant in my blood; do this, whenever you drink it, in remembrance of me.'" Peter held out the plate with pieces of bread toward Ann.

This I will remember: rather than taking one of the small pieces of bread, Ann broke off a sliver, a meagre crumb, of bread, and when we had all taken the elements, Ann dipped the sliver into the grape juice, then placed it on her tongue, where it dissolved. Weeks earlier, she had stopped eating because of the pain; Adrian was now injecting her with morphine every three hours. I took my bread, dipped it in the juice, and we ate. I have always struggled during Communion to experience a palpable sense of Christ's body through a mere morsel of bread and therefore always break off a sizable piece from the loaf, yet at that moment I had a distinct feeling that Christ was very much present in the room, not so much in the bread but more from a sense that it was Christ, in the person of Ann, who lay on the bed.

Later, Adrian would tell me that during this time, when the cancer was in its final stage and had ravaged Ann, she had never appeared to him as beautiful as then. That is a hard thought, and is not intended to make light of Ann's profound suffering, but there is a truth here. Perhaps this is what Dickinson meant when she said,

> Essential Oils—are wrung—
> The Attar from the Rose
> Be not expressed by Suns—alone—
> It is the gift of Screws—,

the sublime process, as Lundin states, through which pain mysteriously produces beauty.

Standing by Ann's bed at that moment we were silent, meditative. After a minute I asked Ann how taking part in Communion in her circumstance affected her experience of the sacrament. She answered by speaking of God's faithfulness and goodness to her. Peter said to Ann, "The next time you take part in Communion will be at the wedding supper of the Lamb, and you will not be ill, but whole."

Peter asked me to say a closing prayer, and though I cannot now recall the words, I do remember it perhaps as the most fervent prayer I have ever said. One cannot be phony at a deathbed. We sang the doxology: "Praise God From Whom All Blessings Flow."

Peter and Adrian rose to bring the Communion elements back to the kitchen, and I was left alone with Ann. She lifted her legs, ever so slowly, and sat on the edge of the bed. I gave her a farewell embrace, the most gentle embrace I have ever given anyone, she looked so small and fragile, and through her nightgown I could feel the bones of her emaciated torso, the brittle bones of a sparrow. I said to Ann, "We love you," "we" meaning Fellowship Church, and Ann said simply, "I know." We said our final goodbye. Inside, I was weeping.

As Peter and I drove home on the Kloets' gravel road we were silent a moment, then spoke of how beautiful this rural part of the city was with all the greenery. Suddenly a black squirrel ran out onto the road and Peter hit the brakes. The squirrel just missed being hit, and ran into the grass at the edge of the road.

A few weeks later, on Wednesday, June 24, a friend phoned the Kloets at 6:00 p.m. to ask how Ann was. She was weak, but still coherent. Adrian and Ann's pastoral elder had arranged to drop by for a visit at seven o'clock that evening . Just after 6:00 p.m., however, Ann died, peacefully. The elder arrived at seven, unaware of Ann's death moments before. In the presence of the family he had chosen to read Psalm 121:

> I lift up my eyes to the hills—
> where does my help come from?

My help comes from the LORD,
The Maker of heaven and earth.
Unbeknownst to him, this psalm had been Ann and Adrian's wedding text.

* * *

Saturday morning, two days after her aneurism, Alice lay in a coma on life support. The family approached Fred Koning, a member of Fellowship CRC and a chaplain at Hamilton General, and requested that Alice be anointed with oil in the presence of church elders according to the Epistle of James. Dick requested that elders Harry Van Dyke and I come. Next day, Fred, Harry and I talked briefly as to the order in which we would pray for Alice. I would introduce us and explain the reason for our visit, Fred would anoint Alice with oil, and Harry would say a closing prayer. That evening, Sunday, December 6 at 8:30 p.m., we drove to the hospital.

Dick and his daughter Carolyn met us in the visitors' lounge of the Intensive Care Unit, and informed us that late that afternoon Alice had taken a turn for the worse. Doctors were worried she was slipping more deeply into a coma. There was some worry that Alice's blood pressure might rise with five of us in the room. We said a brief prayer in the hallway, then Fred led the five of us toward the room where Alice lay. We approached a set of double doors above which, in large blue letters, stood the words "Authorized Personnel Only." The moment we stepped through the doors several nurses working at their stations looked our way, as if to see who had entered this off-limits space. Hospitals already have an aura of solemnity, of crisis and tragedy, and the quick glance of the nurses underscored for me that we were entering restricted territory.

As we entered Alice's room, however, I felt as if I were stepping into a sacred place, a Holy of Holies. The room was dimly lit; a nurse sat behind an instrument board. Alice lay on her back wearing a pale-blue hospital gown, her upper body slightly raised; a coiled white vinyl tube ran from the respirator into her mouth. The machine made a soft blowing noise, its compressor clicking as it gave Alice the air that kept her alive, her chest rising with every rhythmical pump of air. Later Carolyn would tell me that when she had stood in the room the previous day she had regulated her own breathing to match the rhythm of the respirator and that the rhythm was so slow she hardly felt she was getting enough air. Fred stood on one side of Alice's bed, Harry and I on the other; Dick and Carolyn were at the foot of the bed. We stood a moment in silence, in awe, perhaps, at the gravity of the moment.

I was to speak first. I introduced ourselves to Alice, and explained why we had come. I did not know whether she could hear me. Then it was time for the anointing. Fred prayed, then spoke words from the Anglican Church's *Book of Alternative Services*:

> Alice, Through this holy anointing
> may the Lord in his love and mercy uphold you
> by the grace and power of the Holy Spirit. Amen.

Fred took out a small vial of olive oil. Then, like Emily Dickinson's buzzing fly, there came one of those small annoyances that intrude upon a sacred moment. The stopper would not come out of the vial. I watched Fred struggle with it a moment; the vial was an old one and the sponge regulating the flow of oil was apparently worn—until the stopper suddenly came free and the oil, as if it had been confined too long, sprayed from the vial, spattering onto Alice's blue gown. Fred dipped the oil on his index finger and made the sign of the cross on Alice's forehead, dipped oil on his finger again and made the sign of the cross on Alice's right wrist, then on her left. At the foot of the bed, Carolyn reached out her hand to her mother; Dick's arm was around Carolyn's shoulder—members of a family struggling to hang on to one another, to hang on to life. Fred prayed.

When he had finished Harry spoke. He addressed Alice warmly as though she could hear what he was saying, and spoke of her contribution to our church: her work as a deacon, her involvement with Friendship Club. When he was finished Harry said, "Alice, we're going now. We're going to leave you in the hands of Jesus, where you are safe." Then we turned slowly and left the room.

Downstairs we spoke a while with Dick and Carolyn; the nurse had just informed Dick that Alice's blood pressure had not risen at all, which could be either a good sign—our presence had not agitated her—or a bad—she was indeed slipping further away. Both Dick and Carolyn testified they'd felt a powerful sense of peace pervading Alice's room. Carolyn was later to say, in fact, that these moments in room ICU East 6 with the five of us were the most special to her during the whole crisis, more profound even than her mother's funeral.

The following day, Monday, Alice's condition was grave. A nurse informed Dick, in fact, that Alice "would not be coming back." That morning the family decided they would not prolong Alice's life unnaturally by keeping her on life support; they spoke of donating Alice's organs. That decision made, they would not wait in the hospital for Alice's life to ebb away; the monitors showed no brain activity. There was nothing more the family could do for her; in their minds Alice had died already. In Oshawa, two hours' drive away, Debbie was about to give birth; the family decided to be with her and celebrate new life. At five o'clock that afternoon the baby was born.

That evening, chaplain Fred Koning led a brief ceremony. He recited the Lord's prayer, read Psalm 23, then these words from the Gospel of John: "Jesus said to her, 'I am the resurrection and the life. He who believes in me will live, even though he dies; and whoever lives and believes in me will never die.'" He said a prayer declaring God's presence, and for Alice to claim God's promise of life everlasting. He recited a prayer commending and surrendering Alice into God's keeping. Then Alice was taken off life support.

Next day she died.

The words in James' epistle that elders should pray for a sick person, anoint him or her with oil, and that the prayer offered in faith will make the sick person well, do, of course, raise a question. Alice did not get well—was our prayer not offered in faith? I'd like to think it was, although I admit the dilemma. This struggle of faith is one Emily Dickinson knew keenly, and reading her we are perhaps not surprised by how little she says about the efficacy of prayer to save the dying. There are poems that assert Dickinson's lack of fear of death— ". . .for who is He?/ The Porter of my Father's Lodge/ As much abasheth me!"—nevertheless most of Dickinson's emphasis is on the inevitability of death:

> All but Death, can be Adjusted—
> Dynasties repaired—
> Systems—settled in their sockets—
> Citadels—dissolved— . . .
> Death—unto itself—exception—
> Is exempt from Change—.

* * *

Good Shepherd Garden, an oval plot of grass the size of an athletic field but tilted steeply to one side, lies nestled at the foot of the Niagara escarpment. Its greenery has turned brilliant with the spring's ample rain, which has dappled the grass here and there with small brown mushrooms. This plot of grass is a newer part of the cemetery, dotted only here and there with gravestones slightly below the level of the grass, demonstrating the truth of Dickinson's lines,

> The Color of the Grave is Green—
> The Outer Grave—I mean—
> You would not know it from the Field—
> Except it own a Stone—.

The Garden's grassy slope is lined with maples which cast its edges in deep shadow. It is May, and the trees have been in leaf for several weeks. The day, although bright with sun, is still cool with spring. Large clouds float imperturbably across the sky.

Less than a hundred yards away, hidden behind a stand of tall sumac, rises the Niagara escarpment; I can hear but not see the traffic running up and down Highway 403 which climbs the craggy wall of limestone, can hear the throaty growl of truck exhausts audible as the semi-trailers labour to climb the highway's long, steep hill.

Through the steady drone of traffic noise, bird song pierces the blue air. Twenty yards away two young women in track suits stride briskly on the paved drive circling the grass. They talk animatedly. Beyond them a dozen Canada geese waddle silently towards the cemetery's pond where a woman stands feeding the geese bread crusts, their heads at the end of their long black necks dipping again and again into the brilliant green grass. A hundred yards beyond the paved drive, the cemetery's yellow backhoe is digging a fresh grave, its blade clawing hungrily into the earth. The backhoe shudders as it digs. At the funeral tomorrow, green outdoor carpeting will be draped over the mound of dirt.

I resume the search which is the purpose of my visit today, trying to remember the exact spot from when I stood here last more than a year ago, then, after several minutes of exploring, find the two gravestones I'm looking for. They are a mere twenty paces apart, I discover, and have the same appearance: a red granite base bearing a plaque of burnished bronze, the borders of both plaques festooned with garlands of wheat. Both gravestones bear Ann and Alice's Dutch first names.

The first gravestone says, simply,

ANNIGJE KLOET
1943 - 1998

The second bears the inscription

ALDERDINA DEKLEINE
1938 - 1998
BELOVED WIFE OF DIRK

Nearby, one grave bears a brass urn filled with white shasta daisies, another a clutch of yellow carnations surrounding a single purple iris.

The grass over Ann and Alice's graves, as if having had to bear a massive weight, still shows an indentation. But this is no time for pathetic fallacy—it is the soil's own weight that has caused it to sink, I know, the force of gravity that has drawn it into the earth. And yet—*gravis, gravitas*: Latin for heavy, for weight. Gravity. The grave—we are all pulled irresistibly earthward. In one of her short stories Carol Shields states, "Emptiness has weight." If that is so, this emptiness that has weight, *gravitas,* is the emptiness of loss.

Now, however, more than a year after the funerals, I see that the grass over the two graves no longer shows the scars of the backhoe's blade that cut into the earth. The sod, over time, has healed. Just as the heart eventually heals.

As Dickinson words it,

> The Bustle in a House
> The Morning after Death—
> Is solemnest of industries
> Enacted upon Earth—
>
> The Sweeping up the Heart
> And putting Love away
> We shall not want to use again
> Until Eternity.

Scott Moncrieff

POTIPHAR'S WIFE

Day after day she drips
that invitation on Joseph:

a goodly person
and well favored.

I hear her speaking softly,
reclined, lifting a goblet

and eyebrow, Mrs. Robinson
on the Nile, smiling

plastic smiles which harden
on his goodly back.

Scott Moncrieff

GOD'S TUESDAY TO-DO LIST

Old Faithful: 9:45/10:27/11:42 etc.
Meeting w. Angels' Union—travel budgets
Robert's keys, Leticia's history test
Tint adjust/New Hampshire (+ 2%)
Send geese south from Traverse City
Call repair shop re. Gabriel's horn
Lunch w. Moses at Cloud Nine
Discussion group—apocalypse now?
Prevent air disasters: LAX, Heathrow
Sparrow in Murchisons' back yard: 4:30 HST.
Kosovo, Somalia, West Bank, E. St. Louis
Sunset of the week: Mauritius
Supper w. J and Gabriel (ret. trumpet/card)
Call Larry King Live ("Victor from Corpus Christi")
Read Oprah's Book-of-the-Month selection
Turn off Old Faithful

Scott LaCounte

GOLDEN POPPIES

"Six week old baby says '*Solipsism.*'" This was the caption sprawled across the cover of the *National Enquirer.* I was the smiling baby boy under the caption. A Ukrainian comedian turned freelance writer, that my mom was dating at the time, wrote the bogus story. He had promised my mom five hundred dollars to make up the story.

It seems ridiculous to think that there were people who believed that it was true, but there were. After the story was printed, hundreds of letters came addressed to me, a baby, from people who believed in it. One woman said I was the reincarnation of Henry David Thoreau, and she wondered if I had once had a love affair with Emerson; another, the priest of a naturalist church that worked for the conservation of wild chickens in Rhode Island, wrote to say I was the very same child he had seen in a vision, and I was sent to make his church known to the world.

Living is hard when you grow up in a small town where everyone reminds you of the past and everything you didn't want to believe seems to haunt you. When I started school, teachers would always pause at my name when they called roll and ask, "Aren't you that boy that was in the tabloid?" And a month would never pass without someone spotting me in the grocery store and saying, "You're that boy—the one in the tabloid. Was that story really true?"

I wished a lot growing up that the story was true. I used to have dreams that it was—that I had really said solipsism and now led a fairytale life. I was always a genius little boy who could speak complete sentences before his first birthday. People would never say, "aren't you the boy from the tabloid," in this dream—they'd call me by my name and throw in something about being the genius boy. And my mom would love me in these dreams.

When I was nine, my mom told me that she would have to go away to California for awhile and sort some things out. "I just don't know who I am," she told me while she stood in front of her vanity mirror naked plucking at her eyes, "I have to find myself—I have to find my peace. I just don't have the money to take you along."

"Where will I go?"

"Something will come up." For encouragement Mom walked up to me, kissed me on the forehead, and said, "I think your dad is still living in California—maybe we'll get back together."

A week later Mom drove me to my grandma's house in Pergamum, an even smaller town than the one I grew up in, near Albany. I had never met my grandma; I had never seen a picture of her; I had heard her name only a few times.

I can still remember standing on the doorstep to a house I had never been, to see a woman I had never known, and my mom saying, "This is your grandma." Then I was pushed inside and told to wait in the living room. I could hear only vaguely what mom and grandma said. They were arguing—it was something about the past. Finally the door slammed. Mom had left.

I would have cried if I had someone to cry to.

Then Grandma came hobbling into the living room supporting herself with her cane. She stopped in front of me, put on the glasses that hung around her neck by a gold chain, and looked me over carefully. "You have your grandpa's eyes."

I wasn't sure what I was supposed to say, so I scratched my neck (I do this sometimes when I'm nervous).

"If you're going to be staying here, I guess I should show you around." She hobbled out of the room, and I followed behind.

"Your bedroom," Grandma said, opening the door to the first room on her tour. It was simple—bed, dresser, Bible on the nightstand. "It was your mom's room," she said shuting the door before I could look longer.

The bathroom was the second and final room she showed me. "Toilet." Grandma said pointing.

I looked in the bathroom and saw hanging, framed over the toilet, the tabloid magazine with me on the cover.

"That's the only picture I have of you. Your mom sent it to me with a note that said, 'I thought you should know you're a grandma.'"

"Why's it in the bathroom?"

"Because it reminds me whenever I come in here that a lot of crap goes into this world, but eventually that crap will come out. When it does we wipe up, get clean, and go on with our lives."

"Oh," my little voice replied.

"There's a TV in the living room. I'm taking a nap."

I played with the remote control, switching between cartoons and some religious station with a sweaty black man shouting "Jesus" and "road to salvation" in dramatic repetition. I got bored of this after thirty minutes and decided to take my own tour of the house.

Quietly I wandered down the hallway, sliding my hands against the wall as I walked, and quickly peeked my head in each of the open doors. The only room with the light on was the one at the end of the hall. It was Grandma's room.

I stood in the doorframe and watched her. She did not sleep like she said she would. She was kneeling at the side of the bed praying out loud. She prayed for the town, her church, and that she'd grow stronger in faith and love. I giggled a little when she continued to pray that she would win the lottery. Then she let out a deep sigh and prayed for me; she prayed for me to know that she loved me even though she didn't show it much; she prayed that I'd make lots of knew friends while I stayed with her; finally she prayed that I'd find Jesus.

No one had ever prayed for me before.

Making friends was easy in Pergamum because the town was so small and everyone was close. After school about seven or eight of us would always meet. We'd spend the rest of the day pretending we were pirates, space men, soldiers, or spies—I think we had been everything at one point.

One day one of us got the idea that we should try something new—more exciting. For almost a hour we threw out ideas of what we could do. Then someone, I don't remember who, said "How 'bout we play tag in the cemetery?" It got real quiet and no one answered. After a minute of stillness somebody said, "Okay," and we all knew there was no turning back. To say it was a stupid idea would only mean we were too afraid to try it. So for about two weeks, until we got bored again, we played tag at the cemetery.

I was leaving one day when grandma stopped me at the door.

"Did you finish your homework."

I nodded.

"You gonna go down to the old cemetery?" Grandma asked.

"Why would I want to go to the cemetery?"

"I talked to Patti Rosecran at the market. She said boys had been runnin' around playing games down there."

I shrugged my shoulders, "I don't know who they are Grandma."

She carefully eyed me down. I think she knew I was lying, but she nodded anyway. "I don't want to hear 'bout my grandson doing that stuff. Understood?"

I nodded.

"People need to teach their kids to let the dead be."

"Can I go now?"

Grandma finally gave in, "But I want you home by five."

I ran out the door and made it to the graveyard in ten minutes. Everyone was already there. "Did Grandma say it was alright to play?" My best friend, Alex, teased as I joined the rest of the group.

"Shut up."

There was no more talking.

Alex was 'it', and the rest of us had 120 seconds to hide. Brian Rosecran and I ran together until we got to the tombstone of a woman Brian claimed to be his grandma, and we broke up. Brian stayed there, but I kept running.

I found a large tree not much farther from Brian and used its trunk as my shield from Alex. As I caught my breath, I heard the crackling of leaves and turned. A short, skinny, pale-faced, middle aged man in a Hawaiian shirt, stood grinning down at me. "Sure is an odd place for kids to be playing games."

"I'm sorry," I said backing away, "we didn't know anyone was here."

"No worries—you better stay put or your friends are going to find you."

I stayed.

The man lit a small brown cigarette that he was holding, and carefully inhaled.

"Sure is a funny looking cigarette." I didn't know what he was smoking then.

He inhaled deeply, his eyes were wandering, "Yeah."

I could see Alex running, not far from me.

"So you got a name kid?"

"Alex," I lied.

"I live up on that hill over there," The man pointed, "Come down here everyday. I love cemeteries."

"That's a funny thing to like."

"Lot's of people are intrigued by them—look at you and your friends."

"We never said we liked it—it's just a good place to hide."

He nodded, inhaling more of his cigarette. "I feel a certain sense of power when I come to this place. I think of all those people who died, and all the dreams they must have had, but never achieved. Cemeteries are the home of the greatest dreams—you know that?"

I shrugged.

"Everyone has one great dream. Most people never let that dream out though, and it dies with them. That's why I like coming down here—I like to reflect about all those dreams that will never be. What's your great dream, Alex?"

"I don't know."

He closed his eyes and swayed his head to a beat, like he was listening to music. Then he opened them and pointed, "Who's that girl?" She was the only girl in our group. We only let her stay because she was a tomboy and Alex's sister.

"Her names Jessica."

"She's a very pretty girl," He closed his eyes. When they opened this time, I noticed for the first time how glossy they were. He bent down, tore out some grass, then fixed his eyes on it, "Green's a pretty color." He looked back down at me, "Do you think desire is an eternal thing?"

He continued before I answered. "It's all eternal Alex. The trees. The animals. The colors." He paused, closed his eyes, rubbed his hand, then looked back at me and continued his reflection, "I believe in syncretism. Happiness is there—do you know that?"

I scratched my neck and looked in the distance. Alex had spotted Brian. The game was over. "I gotta go mister."

He nodded, "It was nice meeting you Alex—I'm sure we'll meet again."

***

After I lived with grandma longer, we developed a lot of little traditions that I think helped us grow closer together. Saturday mornings we'd eat oatmeal and drink hot cider on the porch. Grandma would tell me funny stories about things her and my grandpa used to do before he died. Sometimes she'd tell me stories about what my mom was like when she was little; I liked those stories most, because mom had never really told me about her past.

One Saturday I asked grandma what happened between her and Mom. Grandma was quiet. I could tell it hurt for her to think about. Finally she said slowly, "Your mom—she was a free spirited child. I never really could control her. When she was seventeen, she got herself pregnant—she never did say who the father was. Me and your grandpa tried real hard to get her to give it up for adoption. We thought that's what she was going to do, but then one day she just left—ran away in the middle of the night.

"I prayed every night for my little girl to come home. Three months later she did, and she wasn't pregnant anymore. Grandpa and her got into a real bad fight, and she left again. Twelve years later she came back with you and left again. Your aunt was able to find her when grandpa died, but she didn't want to come down for the funeral."

"Do you think I'm like her Grandma?"

"You're everything good about her."

From afar, I could see a black Lexus speeding carelessly down the road. It pulled into Grandma's driveway, and I recognized the driver immediately as the man from the graveyard a month back, but I pretended I had never met him. He came out of the car quickly wrapping his arms around his frail body to warm-up, then reached back into the car and pulled out several Golden Poppies bunched together in a rustic bouquet.

He smiled, nodded at Grandma and me on the porch, then jogged towards us. "I'm the Reverend Doctor David Falsus Cambiare." His right arm extended towards Grandma's. Grandma did not shake it.

He turned to me, "And who may you be?" I could tell from his smile that my secret was safe with him.

"My grandson," Grandma said before I could answer, "Why don't you go inside for a while."

I nodded and went quickly inside staying close to the windows. "I brought these for you," I could hear him say. "It's Golden Poppy, the state flower of California. Would you believe I got it to grow in my garden—in this climate!"

"No thanks." Grandma replied, and I could hear the flowers hit the ground.

"Yes, well, I just wanted to introduce myself. You of course know about my church down the street."

"I've heard some talk."

"It will have its first service a week from Sunday, and I wanted to offer you my personal invitation."

"I go to church in town."

"The United Methodist on Main?"

I peeked out the window and could see Grandma nodding.

"Then you haven't heard? Next month we'll be combining our congregations and meeting as one."

Grandma said nothing.

"We'll be joined as brothers and sisters, becoming one spirit."

I think he felt uncomfortable around grandma, so he decided to leave. "I'll look forward to seeing you again." He tried again to shake Grandma's hand, but she again refused it.

I waited until I saw the reverend's car pull out of the driveway, then I went back out to the porch. "Who was that man grandma?"

"He's no concern of yours."

"I sat back down next to her on the porch. "You think they'll really close down your church grandma?"

"You were listening in on me?"

I shrugged my shoulders and shamefully nodded.

She shook her head, "You have to learn some manners."

"Sorry," I mumbled, "Is it true though?"

"I don't know."

Grandma was a legend in her town history. She had served on almost every church committee, baked something in all the county fairs, and even had ran for mayor one year (that was the same year Grandpa got cancer, and she dropped out of the race before the election was held, though everyone says she would have won). She was well respected in church, led a Bible study, and was head of the prayer chain. She knew everyone and had a say in everything important.

Two nights before the pastor and his wife had come over for dinner. For almost two hours they had talked about the church and its congregation—he even asked grandma's advice on what to do about some of the church's problems. At no point was there any mention of the church merging or even the new minister, David Falsus Cambiare, though they both knew about him. She had no say in that matter.

Grandma was always serious—like she was on a mission. She was sad that day.

* * *

The minister did not give a sermon on Sunday. He rambled on for about ten minutes about a lack of church finances. Then he did the unthinkable—the unforgivable of any church pastor—he proclaimed that he no longer believed. He had not lost faith in Christ, he had lost faith in the Methodist denomination and all its Christian traditions. He finished by saying, "I'm tired of the disputes and controversies. I've taken a position at the Community Worship Center, and I'm asking all of you to abandon the church with me." Then he left the pulpit.

When the minister walked out, the church became eerie quiet. Grandma and I were sitting in the second to front row; it was so quiet that I could even hear Peter Jonson's dad, some twenty pews back whisper, "*Oh crap*," as the minister walked out.

For three days, the new and old minister went to each member of the church, there were about fifty who came each Sunday, and personally convinced almost the entire congregation to go to the new church. Only Grandma and a few others said they would stay. By the end of the week everyone knew there was no finances to keep the church alive, and it would be forced to close.

The next Sunday Grandma got me up early.

"Are we going to the new church?"

Grandma nodded yes.

"I thought you didn't like the pastor there."

"We have to give everyone their chance I guess."

We made it as far as the parking lot of the new church the next Sunday, but we never went in. From her car we sat and looked. The church was twice the size of the old church, but it did not resemble a church. There was no steeple, stain glass, bells to call worship, or even a cross to say Christ is welcomed here; it was round, with a dome-like ceiling. Near the front doors a large sign stood tall with the church's name, the sermon, and the pastor—"Community Worship Center" it read in big bold letters, followed by smaller print, "What God Doesn't Want Us To Know, by the Reverend Doctor David Falsus Cambiare." Next to the sign was Cambiare, wearing a yellow robe and thongs.

Grandma wouldn't go to church there—Grandma couldn't go to church there.

She left the parking lot, then the town, never saying anything to me.

"Where we going Grandma?"

"To church."

"How come you didn't like the new church?"

"Because it wasn't a church."

"Oh."

She continued driving east, past churches of science, temples for gods, and even one that simply read church, which we discovered was a place for people who did not believe in God or a god, but liked the idea of church.

Fifteen miles out of town, we saw a sign, hidden shamefully behind poorly trimmed bushes, which read 'Sunday Message.' She could not make out what the message was but knew for sure it had one. There was a small church hidden behind tall oak and pine trees.

It was nondenominational and had only about twenty members. Everyone seemed a little uncomfortable at our presence. We sat in the back and listened for twenty minutes to a man strum praise hymns on an out of tune guitar, then the pastor delivered his message. I don't understand a lot of sermons but his was simple and pretty easy to follow. Grandma said she liked it, and I was certain we'd be back the next Sunday.

When we came back into town after church, Pergamum seemed different— changed. Children and adults alike ran wildly in the streets with no direction. There was chaos and a lack of order. I knew some of the faces that ran the streets, and I waved when we past them—nobody waved back.

At home grandma went to her bedroom, shut the door, the window, and the curtains. I left her alone, but inside her room I could hear her crying, praying, then crying some more.

That night it was muggy and rained a little. There was a leak on the roof, and I used a pan to catch the water. The roof was falling apart. The entire house was falling apart.

***

The Saturday of the first snowfall I sat on the porch with grandma, but we didn't tell stories. "Have you ever heard the sound of snow melting?"

"No Grandma."

"I love that sound. It's so soothing and comforting. It's a hard sound to hear—you have to be real quiet—but it's worth it. You know when you hear it that how ever hard the winter was there's hope—there's warm weather soon."

"Will you tell me the next time you hear it Grandma so I can hear it to?"

"I can't hear it any more."

I looked up at her, and I could see a tear rolling from her eye.

"It's okay grandma."

There was a tear in her other eye, "Maybe there's just no more to hear."

Grandma's close friend, Margaret Hatcher, died of a stroke the next day. The Reverend Doctor David Falsus Cambiare called bringing her the news and telling her when the service would be to release her spirit from her body.

Grandma thought about going to the service, but the church haunted her. She did not go.

***

Months turned to years. For awhile we would go out of town for church, then Grandma stopped going altogether. The trip out of town became too much for her. On Sundays, Grandma would read her Bible and I would sleep in.

When I was sixteen, I went to the Community Worship Center. It was more peer pressure then curiosity (though there was some of that). All my friends went there, and it became odd that I did not do the same.

I didn't like it. The first part of the service someone played Celtic music, then someone read announcements—mediation class on Monday, a seminar class taught by the old Methodist minister called "Understanding Your Spiritual Self" on Wednesday morning, a more advanced seminar Thursday night called simply "Acosmism," and Saturday a ladies breakfast. There was no sermon; instead there was what the minister called "Words To Reflect," and that day he was reflecting two things: first, whether or not there was more than one way to heaven; and second, did he believe in a theory he called Adoptianism—his answer to both was yes. It was too complex to understand most of it, and I didn't like him as a minister, but the next Sunday I went back.

I think I just felt like a lot of people that went to church there—welcomed. Grandma did not talk to me a lot any more. She was dying. But I also wanted to know about spirituality—I wanted to know the force that made Mom leave me, and Grandma so strong; the Community Worship Center was the place I thought I had to go to find that.

Grandma found out I was going to the church a month later. The reverend had called up to invite me on a youth retreat while I wasn't home and gave Grandma the message.

"Reverend Doctor David Falsus Cambiare called," she said when I walk through the door.

"Oh."

"What made you go there?"

"It was just my friends were all going, and—I don't know. I just went."
She nodded, then slowly walked back into her room.
I followed behind her, "I was going to tell you Grandma."
She didn't answer. I felt guilty.
"Don't be mad at me Grandma—I don't even like the church."
This time she did turn around, "You look like your mother more every-day." She turned back around and looked out the frosted window, "Does anyone ask about me anymore when you go out, or do most people figure I'm dead?"

***

The first day of Spring, a Friday, just as the sun rose, Grandma died.

I found her when I went to tell her I was leaving for school. I got on my knees and said a prayer for her like she had said for me the first day we met.

The minister from the last church Grandma had ever gone to held a small service for her at his church fifteen miles away. Only a few people showed up. My aunt drove down from Buffalo for the service and to pick me up. My mom had arranged for me to stay with her until I started college. In the back row the Reverend Doctor David Falsus Cambiare sat; he left before the service was over.

At her burial, a single Golden Poppy was put on her grave, with a small piece of paper signed by the Reverend Doctor David Falsus Cambiare that said, "*Agape* and *Eros*."

Grandma's house was sold and torn down. My aunt sold most her other stuff at a garage sale and donated what was left to the church. My aunt told me I could have anything I wanted. I kept her Bible.

A lot of things have changed sinse Grandma died. I heard the Reverend Doctor David Falsus Cambiare's church has grown even more. Mom moved up to Oregon—she tells me she's close to finding herself spiritually. And me? I'm...

Often I'll rub my fingers across Grandma's name, inscribed on the front page of her Bible. It makes me feel close to her sometimes, but mostly it reminds me that she's dead. It's dead. I wonder about my own life—my own spiritual self. I wonder what they'll say when I die—"that boy—the one from the magazine". Maybe they'll even call me by my name.

Kathryn R. Campbell

ANAMNESIS

We celebrated the Eucharist at my
house last Thursday. America calls this holyday

Thanksgiving. Our community gathered:
myself, my husband, two daughters, sister, brother-in-law, niece, and now a

Son. Boyfriend of the younger daughter also ate
with us, as have other friends in other years. All are

Welcome. My older daughter and I set the table
together using candles and organdy left over from her August

Wedding. We remembered how it looked that
night when we feasted around that same

Table. Three months had already passed since that
mythical occasion and this familiar family ritual helped us to not

Forget. From a circle of hands and hearts, our prayer of
gratitude mingled with our laughter, the ground we stood on

Sacred. There was the blessing and the breaking, the
giving and the taking of bread, wine, smiles, and

Memories. Remember when Mom took us to Luby's in
'91 and tried to convince us it was just as good as being at

Home. (It wasn't.) We needed mincemeat pie just like Grandmother Katie
made when James was a boy. We needed the smell of turkey in the

Air. We needed a double layer of marshmallows so
Brooke didn't have to eat any of the sweet potatoes

Underneath. We needed our dishes, our turkey napkins, our music and
our flowers, those outward and visible signs of an inward and spiritual

Grace. This year we shared all of these and more, adding a key lime pie for
the new son-in-law. In peace and love we had

Communion.

SuzAnne C. Cole

A LAMENT FOR OUR DAUGHTERS

Weep for Jephthah's daughter,
slender sandalled feet dancing a welcome,
singing celebration for a father's conquest,
she becomes his sacrifice for victory.
Submitting, she begs only one small boon,
two months to mourn her virgin womb,
before offering up herself, obedient, nameless.

Weep for Iphigenia,
slaughtered on the altar of a father's pride.
Army assembled, ships harbor-stalled,
Agamemnon harkens to Calchas:
Artemis must have blood.
Gag her, bind her, spill her
scarlet blood upon the sand.
The fleet sails for glory and for Greece.

Weep for all the daughters of patriarchy:
Missing girl found raped and strangled;
Father charged with sexual abuse.
Tender bodies turned inside out
sucked dry of sweetness,
pulp stripped away by ravenous teeth,
empty rinds chucked aside.

Weep, women, for all our daughters.

SuzAnne C. Cole

POTIPHAR'S WIFE REPLIES

(Genesis 39)

What if I said I had no children
and thus no value in Egypt?
No excuse.

What if I said I was miserably bored,
thought Isis sent the handsome slave?
No excuse.

What if I said desire flooded my body like
the Nile in spring flux through mud levees?
No excuse.

What if I said "lie with me" was all I
could gasp through heavy honey-hot days?
No excuse.

What if I said I followed Potiphar's wishes,
who placed all he owned in Joseph's hands?
No excuse.

What if I said the rest of my life was
dust and flies, isolation and monotony?
No excuse.

What if I said I was merely the ladder
the dreamer used to become second to Pharaoh?

Jeffrey De Lotto

A VISIT TO BUCHENWALD CAMP

On a brilliant sunny Spring day in 1993, the Thuringian hills loud with the sounds of birds, I crunched across gravel fine as bread crumbs. Set in stone walls, topped by an innocuous green clapboard room and short clock tower, the wrought iron gate held a simple cast inscription: "Jedem das Seine" (each to his own). Through these gates had been marched over a quarter of a million people, eighty thousand of whom would never leave alive.

I hadn't even planned to go, taking a break from a Fulbright Lectureship in American literature at Plovdiv University in Bulgaria, but Leipzig had been a disappointment. Much of Eastern Europe had been a surprise, not in many ways pleasant. Oh, I had seen the photos in *Newsweek*, had read the articles about indigenous minorities, but I wasn't prepared for the Gypsy ghettos in Bulgaria, wasn't prepared for the gangs of dark children younger than eight roving the markets and shops, stealing oranges and light switches and openly breathing lacquer thinner from crumpled paper bags. I wasn't prepared for the Gypsy beggars and shell games, wads of soiled currency on the paving stones, nor for the attitudes voiced by many Bulgarians: "They are animals, dirty thieves, all of them. Exterminate them—they are parasites, vermin!" It all seemed so pre-World War II, right out of an old Hollywood movie.

That was my problem (and I don't think I'm alone in this)—so much of what I thought and believed of Eastern Europe was a movie world, the reality carefully concealed from the West.

As a cautious American, I flew over Serbia that year for obvious reasons, landing in Budapest, and took a series of efficient trains to Leipzig, crossing first into the new Czech Republic and then into what had so very recently been a very Soviet East Germany, crossing previously frightening borders with a careless wave from the guards moving through, after they saw our U.S. passports. And so after changing trains in Dresden, all signs of the bombing long gone, I stepped off the train in the Leipzig bahnhof, a polished football stadium of a station, one lone uniformed worker riding a slow floor buffer over a wide expanse of immaculate concrete. Almost at the doors, a huge glistening head, a bizarre vending machine of some type drew our attention; after a mark was fed into the box and "English" was selected for language, the machine rang out, "I am the mouth of truth! Place your hand in my mouth." The mouth-shaped opening was at about waist level, but sudden visions from grade B horror movies and old *Twilight Zone* episodes made me hesitate.

My hand slid forward into the hole and a dull red glow emanated from the opening. "Keep your hand in my mouth!" the machine commanded, and a moment later continued, "Read what I have said!" as a slip of paper dropped into a basket below. The paper read: "WHAT VIRTUE," but without a question mark...a simple enough message, but leaving me both disturbed and dissatisfied.

After a very expensive dinner of schnitzel in a chrome and glass cafe and a glimpse of prosperous new shops and natty occupants, I resolved to try again the next day but had no better luck—there were some old shops peddling antiques, but just table linens, doilies, old cocktail clothes from the thirties—nothing wartime, nothing with the sense of history or disturbance about it, nothing of that old Leipzig I had dreamt was still lurking here somewhere. As in Bulgaria, any sense of a country existing before 1950 had been carefully swept and scrubbed away.

Finally, inspired but ignorant, I marched to a clean new travel service, snickering beforehand to hide our discomfort at what I knew would be a horrible question any way I put it, and plopped down in front of a flashy blonde young man in pleated trousers and a green silk tie: "Where is the nearest concentration camp?" I asked. "Is one nearby?" I tried to sound as though I were asking for directions to a pastry shop.

He cheerily directed me to a map, showed me how to get a train to Weimar, and informed me I needed to get a bus to Buchenwald from there.

I knew nothing about "Konzentrationslager Buchenwald" except a vague reputation, though the thick pamphlet I picked up at the Headquarters Building set an ominous tone, and I strode out on the guided walking tour, beginning along "Karacho-weg," the road prisoners marched along past the Political Section, where the Gestapo decided on sentences and interrogated prisoners.

However, as I wandered along reading, the sense of a very politicized view began to grow. Weimar is described as "well known all over the world for its great traditions of bourgeois humanism." Several pages later, the pamphlet indicates that many "SS barbarians from Buchenwald went unpunished in the western zones of occupation in Germany," the Soviet voice, and I flipped back to the second page, noting the 1986 printing date, again feeling the tension of history, the awkward shift of alliances, the unresolved struggle and resentment of victor and captive that I had felt and seen as I neared these gates.

It had begun in the Thuringian town of Naumburg, where I had taken a taxi on to the next town and had seen on the rim of enclosing hills, as the road wound along the deep valley cut by the Saale River, what looked like giant squat red-brick lighthouses. The driver, one of the ubiquitous unshaven Middle Easterners who seem to drive most of the world's taxis, understood my interest, driving up through the steep switchback streets lined with solid brick and plaster houses and apartments to the summit: a series of immense but derelict industrial windmills for grinding grain—wonders of powerful architecture and abandoned machinery, giant gears and housings thick with grease, quiet as an abandoned child's toys. I groped over the ruins, having clamored over a chain-link fence like the unruly American I was, out of sight of the driver, but bored I quickly returned to the car.

Just before the old blue sedan began to hum down toward Bad Kosen, a series of solidly built apartment blocks shaded by landscaped trees hove into view around a turn, but I noticed that the windows were broken out, doors ajar, black graffiti, swastikas, obscenities, painted on walls and doors.

"What's this?"

"Russians lived here," the thickset driver said. "They had everything of ours—money, good jobs, everything! They took whatever they wanted, treated us like shit...Thank God they are gone."

And I could taste the bitterness, the hatred, of oppression like a pill caught in the back of my throat. A quite different feeling came over after waiting on a bus bench for half an hour and stepping onto the bus I thought was headed for the camp.

"Buchenwald?" I asked.

"Ja, ja!" the driver snapped at me glaring, and after I extended a handful of marks, he grabbed what he needed and waved me back. The middle-aged man, heavy-set with a short haircut and pressed white uniform shirt, obviously did not like me or want me on his bus, but was it because he was an old nationalist who thought I was one of a series of recent conquerors who were blaming his country for what happened in the war? Or was it because he had advanced himself with the Soviets and blamed me for initiating his decline in power? I didn't have time to find out from the man, though this was an often-encountered dilemma for me. In a way I didn't mind him as much as those wonderfully helpful and welcoming folks I worked with in Bulgaria (and I'm sure they are far from few) who I later learned from others had been American-hating die-hard old communists just five years earlier.

Beyond the gatehouse at Buchenwald, a wide downward sloping field stretched out toward a distant three-story factory-looking building, with two smaller masonry buildings to the right side, but the entire central expanse of where the camp had been—hospital, the block where "medical experiments" had taken place, all the barracks, where over forty buildings had stood—was swept clean and bare. But this was not a peaceful and pastoral field but a scraped, a razed ruin of surface tagged with spaced markers, gravel broken with patches of green weeds this bright Spring day, tiny yellow broom flowers spraying the tips with color.

And as I looked over the stark black and white photographs of Roll Call Square and of the expanse of where those fifty blocks of barracks buildings had stood, again I felt the wind sweeping across the scraped and barren ground, thinking, why were *all* those buildings cleaned away? Why not *some* left to make us know what it must have been?

But I walked on, trod on really, since walking was just too casual for the heavy pall of history that lay all about me like a fog, the sun shining brightly down nonetheless, ridiculously, its warmth and light meaningless, useless here.

The camp crematorium squatted near the concrete perimeter fence posts curving inward like claws, rusted barbed wire still hung, loosely, like strands of old hair. Built in 1940 to manage the sharp increase of bodies, the thick red-brick chimney and ovens underneath sat above a cold, damp stone basement lined with heavy pairs of meat hooks six feet off the floor. But all that whitewash could not keep the stink of mortality from oozing through, and I swam up the stairs out of an oil of spirits.

Light flooded the long room where a row of iron-bound ovens gaped, iron rails set into the floor leading up to each door. This, I thought, this is the mouth of truth, and remembered the rasping sound of that hideous plastic head back in the Leipzig train station.

Out in the sunlight nearby, a twelve-foot pole rose into what must be an innocent blue sky, as it and others like it had stood, with prisoners hoisted by their hands chained behind their backs those many years ago. A low wagon with two iron wheels rested alongside, half full of jagged stones. The cart had often been loaded with up to five tons of rock, pulled by prisoners who were beaten with sticks by SS guards (the guards derisively called these people "singing horses").

"Never again!" I heard, the cry seeming to rise from the gravel at my feet. As I rose to go, opening the pamphlet to see where next to turn my steps, that second smaller leaflet I had picked up fluttered down. What could this possibly add to my feeling of loss, of disappointment, about the inhumanity of humanity?

The bold print headings of this folded paper entitled "Buchenwald Memorial" stopped my feet in mid-stride: **Buchenwald Concentration Camp 1937-1945**, and then the second heading: **Buchenwald Special Camp No. 2 1945-1950**. The second set of dates I suppose should have shocked me more, but I was only angry with what I knew to be our willful ignorance.

Reminded that groups of armed prisoners had helped liberate themselves on April 11, 1945, as the camp came under attack from the U.S. Third Army, I again read the oath taken by former prisoners mustered on the parade ground, April 19, 1945: "We will only give up the fight when the last guilty parties stand before the peoples' judges! Our maxim is the annihilation of Nazism root and branch. Our aim is the building of a new world of peace and freedom." And that sounded so promising, until the story that followed, until the reminder of the Yalta Conference, where somebody we fondly called "Uncle Joe" and the Red Army had been given this half of Germany.

The Soviets had apparently released the last 21,000 remaining prisoners by mid-August to return to their countries. However, the occupying Soviets immediately began using Buchenwald as an internment camp for "denazification," redesignating it Special Camp No. 2 and filling it with various people rounded up by the NKVD, another Gestapo but with a red star in lieu of a swastika.

According to recent reports, only a small portion of the prisoners were persons found to be guilty under Allied Control Council Directive 38. Others were "lower and medium-rank Nazi functionaries, functionaries of the Hitler Youth organization, youths detained under the so-called Werewolf suspicion, public employees, industrialists, but also people opposed to the social changes in the Soviet zone of occupation after 1945." That last group was obviously very nebulously defined. The total interned during those years is estimated to be approximately 32,000, of whom somewhere between 8,000 and 13,000 died of

"hunger, diseases, epidemics and in consequences of bad accommodations."
A third of the inmates—dead of "bad accommodations."

What went on in Buchenwald *after* World War II? I do not have any confidence we will ever fully know, especially since a more orderly withdrawal from what became Buchenwald Special Camp No. 2 has made history very difficult to unearth; "documentation proves difficult," the authorities have said, and nothing was publicly memorialized for this *post-war* Buchenwald "until the radical social change in the GDR in 1989 [when] in memory of victims of special camp no. 2 a place of mourning and remembrance was arranged, as yet provisionally, on the northern slope of Ettersburg where many of the dead were buried in mass graves."

The wind stirred the tufts of grass and yellow broom pushing up from a pile of loose rubble where I had wandered near the back of the compound. Broken white tiles were mixed in with gray-brown soil, between where had once stood the prisoners' hospital and Block 46, a building for "medical experiments." How long did experiments continue? We will never know, but let us not forget that this place, the barbarity of this place did not end with 1945, nor does it end today.

Jeanette Hardage

DIVINE SERVICE

There it was—
an impossible cleanup job
accomplished.

I more than tithed the Waiter.
Still, it hardly seemed enough
for service beyond
all reasonable hope.

James Hoggard

THE DRAW OF DARKNESS

When bursts of wind make seasons shift
the sun sometimes burns clouds away
and the sky becomes a blinding blue
so startling that we turn away

Sometimes when sun burns clouds away
explosions of light become so bright
the sky becomes a blinding blue,
and seeking refuge from the light—

the flash and glare of it so bright—
we have to turn our eyes away
And as we try to hide from light
we discover that darkness draws us—

we welcome the way it pulls us—
and admitting that light frightens us
we confess that darkness draws us
when bursts of wind make seasons shift

James Hoggard

TWILIGHT

Before the neighborhood street lamps come on
it's almost dark enough to think the world
might be a shadow of God, although at dusk
there's still enough light left to let me think
night might become the day's erotic twin,
that slopes of thigh and underthigh might lead
to sighs and moans that lead to speech,
to words that lips and arms and fingers speak
when I assume a sacramental solitude

Alan P. R. Gregory

MEDITATIONS FROM BLANK

Blank, Texas, is about forty-four miles east of Dallas. I spent a night there once. Most of us want to avoid Blank: it's the quintessence of nowhere. A random, wretched, shabby huddle, fallen by the highway: gas station, general store, Dairy Queen, a few abandoned cars, empty dumpsters, and the Blank motel. The sort of ugliness it takes years to create. No one admits to coming from Blank: "Oh, somewhere in Texas," they say, "near Dallas." If you're born in Blank, you need an alibi. Short of birth, how do you end up in Blank? By accident, I imagine-a perverse concatenation of vocational devils. Whatever the sad catastrophe, you probably hush it up. You took a turn and there you were. The sad girl in the Dairy Queen pats your arm. Perhaps she thinks, "another lost soul." She says, "have a nice day." And it sounds like a curse.

My night in Blank was entirely unplanned. A new job had my wife and me leaving Atlanta for Austin in June 1995. We traveled in convoy: Suzy in the Jeep with the parrot while I led the way in a 23-year-old Pontiac with a dog and two cats. After 800 miles of uneventful road, the Pontiac coughed, shook a bit, and died. I got out and stood on the roof. Strewn by the highway, about two miles off was Blank, Texas. The dog, two cats, and I squeezed into the jeep. Suzy drove to the gas station. After arranging for a tow, I left my car in the hands of a long-term manic-depressive named Billy Bob.

Over in the Blank Motel, an Asian lady in a sari sat at the desk watching a Brazilian soap opera.

"I'd like a room," I said.

She spotted Suzy getting out of the car. "One hour or two?" she asked.

"Oh no." I panicked. "You don't understand. I'm a priest. I need all night."

She clearly thought I was flattering myself. "Well, as you're a priest," she smiled winningly, "you get the discount - all night for the two hour rate."

I think she'd done this before. I imagined a stream of ministers—Methodists, Pentecostals, revivalist clergy, Episcopalians—all slipping down to Blank for the naughty discount on their off nights. *Don't know what the church is coming to*, I thought as I opened the car. The Indian lady watched us through the office window, and she frowned as I unloaded the dog, parrot, and two cats. Clearly, she was pondering their sexual destiny.

Around nine, I trudged over to the gas station. My Pontiac was in bits, lots of bits, the "well-we-can't-remember-where-this-goes-so-we'll-leave-it-out-and-hope-it-doesn't-matter" sort of bits. Billy Bob was amusing his friends squirting gasoline into the carburetor with a water pistol. This is probably irrational prejudice, but I couldn't help remembering that the ranks of Space Shuttle designers and open-heart surgeons were pretty thin on men named Billy Bob.

"Failed fuel pump," he said. "I put a mechanical in, but it ain't working, so's you better have electric."

"Is that expensive?"

He then offered to buy the car.

"Do you realize," I said grimly, "that not only do I have a strong emotional attachment to this vehicle but this is my only, my absolutely only way out of sunny Blank."

Eleven o'clock next day I paid for the electric pump. We left, Billy Bob still raising his offer for the car. Forty miles later I broke down outside a truck stop in Dallas. Blank, Texas has a long shadow.

Elijah fled...he went on for forty days and forty nights to Horeb, the mount of God. He entered a cave and there he spent the night (1 Kings 19:8-9).

Dearest Belladonna,

I checked into this hotel soon after breakfast. From the window, I can see the mountain, its edges as hard as your heart. I'm not sure this will reach you, if it does, though, I'm certain you won't want to read it. Seeing, however, that you have cast me off and that I cannot even remember the name of this hotel, receive it, my dear, as a postcard from nowhere, about nothing, from nobody. Outside, the olive trees climb the mountain, stopping only at a snow line— cool like you. The sun throws white fire through their gray-green leaves. Soil glints, bark crackles, fences glow. My heart, however, catches nothing. Don't be misled by the way I've filled this card. In truth, it remains—like my heart— a blank. I write only because I cannot stand being so damn speechless.

Farewell, your loving,

Elijah.

The night before my mother died, the surgeons removed one of her lungs. Before the operation, my father visited. He sat by the bedside. "It's late," she said. "You shouldn't have come." They talked of this and that; about his day; the flowers she'd been sent; a kindly nurse. Not about the lung, or the short passage to death, or the fear. On an old map, beyond the borders of the land where town and village, river and hill is named, it says "Here are the speech-less lands." The rest is blank. The monitor beeped by the bedside. Downstairs, the operating theatre was prepared. Up here, though, we did not talk of how they will lift the lung from her chest; of how desperate it all is; of thirty years loving and living, soon past. "It's late," she said, "You shouldn't have come."

"It's no trouble." He patted her shoulder. The words are cover stories, alibis, if you will: "we are not here, really"—my mother, my father deny their presence, caught in the speechless lands, the silent wastes of the blank.

A newspaper article tells me that the greenhouse effect is worse than any-one realized, dooming us by mid-century. In another, drownings and ruin, a woman up to her breasts in mud. These truths have such a little life. I send them on their way into silence, gliding on excuses, vain reasonings, distrac-tions. I catch them, only for a moment, out of the corner of my eye, as they recede, vanishing into the blank: that extended and extensive sphere of all I am afraid to voice, don't want to name, don't want to give room, give the life of speech. This far country, land of forgetfulness, ruled by the politics of anxious sanity, sweet rationality, the haunts of what we fear to name, the world we speak of not at all or only in the cool whisper of reason: this land is vast. Outside, there is the world we deny—and, inside, the heart we evade. For our hearts, too, have their blanks, zones of the unspoken, full of emptiness, the dead halls of the unattended. The memory we cannot face, the unacknowledged fear that haunts us, the sin unforgiven, the loss we cannot bear to reckon: inside and out, we are besieged by the unspeakable.

And there was an earthquake, but the Lord was not in the earthquake (1 Kings 19:11).

Dearest Belladonna,
    I know why this room came cheap. There's a railroad under the window. Train came through after lunch. Damn near shook me off the bed. Rumbling, screeching, walls bending out, ceiling dropping plaster, bed howling at the joints. But I want you to know this, Belladonna. I lay here like a stone. Not a flicker in this wasted soul. Nothing to that turbulence. Nothing to fill this heart. Nothing to break the silence, not even to voice a moment's rage.
                                        Farewell, your loving,
                                            Elijah.

We cannot—or so we're taught—say what God is in himself; we can only say what God is not. God is, finally, unspeakable. Perhaps. But perhaps, also, it is not enough to say that: perhaps that is not yet the gospel, not yet the disturbance, the unsettlement we need, not yet the redemption. Perhaps this unspeakable God is yet truly the most communicable reality: from the beginning Word, voiceable, eager for articulation in flesh and blood. Perhaps the problem is mostly ours. Perhaps we would rather not be with God where and when God speaks, where and when he becomes what he most truly is—communicable, love, Word. "Who could have believed what we have heard?" asks the prophet. "Where has the power of the Lord been revealed? His form was disfigured, beyond recognition. Foul beyond words. We despised him, turned away our eyes. He became a curse for us, not even to be whispered in good company. Come, look away, talk of other things, of this and that but not...not him. Pierced, tormented, struck down. Who has words for this? We assigned him a grave in silence, in the land of forgetfulness, in the blank." In the center of history, there is the unspeakable. A conspiracy of silence. We have put it there, fleeing from our neighbor and from ourselves, covering the tracks of our violence, creating a vast and silent blank for all—inside and outside us—all that falls by the wayside. "We held him of no account but yet he was pierced for our transgressions." Where the fear, the horror, the grief is cordoned off by our evasions, and alibis, and cover stories, here, God voices himself, naming the unnamed as the house of his dwelling, the transformation of nowhere. In the center of history, in the unspeakable, voiceless blank, *there* is the Unspeakable God, speaking words of mercy, speaking himself. The Word, filling in the blank. This is the gospel. Remember that Transfiguration? On the mountain, they watch his glory: his smile on Moses, his arm around Elijah. To and fro in the glory, talking of Exodus, mapping the way into the unnamed country, that near and distant wilderness: the unrecognized neighbor and the uncried pain—the blank.

And then a still small voice (I Kings 19.13).

Dearest Belladonna,

Forgive me. Woke up this morning, banged the jug by the bedside, spilt water all over myself, soaked. Slumped back on the bed, knocked the Gideon Bible off the shelf above my head. It hit me full in the face, and lay across my nose, like a raft. It was the end, Belladonna. I didn't move, just stayed there, cursing the day I was born. Damn, damn, damn, damn, damn, damn, damn. Swearing like the bell tolls, damn, damn, damn. Then, Belladonna, underneath, I heard my heart—like a stranger, tapping. Damn, damn, damn...tap, tap, tap. My empty heart, speaking as it filled, filling like a shell fills with the sea. The Spirit on Exodus into the blank heart, the heart singing in its still small voice. Dry husk of a soul, watered, blooming. Blank no more, Belladonna, no more that claustrophobic, scrunched up, self-pitying, damnable silence. I whined good, didn't I? White noise—signifying nothing. But believe me, my love, this card is full, really full, written on the inside and the out. Like the scroll of God, Belladonna. Opened, shouting from the rooftops.

Goodbye, your loving,

Elijah.

"Then the Spirit drove him into the wilderness." With wild beasts and a coagulating silence. There he sat, singing softly, and summoning angels, laying the foundations in his own flesh, of a new fellowship. Here begins the Church: a community of courage. A community, as we say, of the Word, the Word that breaks the silence. For, God knows, we have had enough of silence; we are dying of the quiet politics of sanity, from keeping our heads. We need, desperately, the madness of one singing in the desert, crying out our woes, shouting the names of the ignored and the wretched. "It's late," she said. "You shouldn't have come." No! You should have come and you should have clung together howling your woe to the Most High. There is too much silence. Too much turning away. Too much is left unsaid, far too much evil left without protest, too much we cannot admit to ourselves, even from the stores of our own hearts. Too little reality finds a voice in us, in our imaginations, in our loving.

So where do we find God? In the wilderness, in the speechless lands calling us to join him. The Spirit drove him into the wilderness. Why? That we might make of the wilderness a city full of speech. Because men and women are called to make Exodus, to be with God in the deserts of the blank, learning how to break its silence, learning how to speak. Discovering how to articulate the world, in words and deeds to articulate the world as a world beloved, a world being formed in the Divine mercy. We have to practice the language that transforms a wilderness of silence: forgiveness, lament, naming evil, love, welcome, recognition, thanksgiving—and praise, praise for the God who sets the silent halls of the dead a buzzing with voices.

For this, the Spirit makes Exodus into our trembling hearts. Brooding, tender and fierce, forming the courageous soul, opening the stopped mouth that has become a tomb for hope, freeing the tongue. It is in this Holy Spirit that we discover freedom of speech—and the life it lets us in for. Honestly, I find this prospect, the prospect of confronting the unsayable, of resisting my fearful desire for silence: I find this prospect as daunting as I do hopeful—almost. The alternative, after all, the alternative is illusion, idle chatter, silent embarrassment, words without Word; striking ourselves dumb. The alternative to learning the liberating speech of God is to live our lives as alibis, denying our presence in the unspeakable, settling for sorry distractions, shuffling in the line, queuing in the Blank motel for that seductive, ministerial discount.

Mary Harwell Sayler

CHECKOUT DESK
AT THE LIBRARY

Your name calls me
across the ages
of distant stars
& closed embankments
of cribs & crevices,
crypts & caverns
beyond the pages
& typed pages
of historical bliss
& abysses
into the unguarded
tongue of a garden
where names are named,
and in some book
of life or poem,
your Word translates
me into a closer
reading of
infinity.

Mary Harwell Sayler

ODD ANGLES

Lord, I can't begin to know
how much you suffer,
                    suspended
there:
an artifact on my wall.

What do you detect in me
as I reflect on this unlikely
fact of art
found
in a crucifix?

How can I keep you
elevated & not
just
          hanging
around
with nothing to do but

balance
the cross
     points
          of my life?

Mary Harwell Sayler

OUTLINING THE CONTEMPORARY

What is this love of things, temporal
and temporary, but, oh, contempt
for contemplation within the temple
of the soul?

Press a palm
to the forehead's temple,
and trace the lifeline's curve
from all temptation toward
The Way of tempering even
the most temperamental temperament.

Yes! This
is the one true template:
Christ's stencil
etched in us – ever
contemporary.

J. Paul Holcomb

WILD ASS SONNET

(Luke 19:29-46)

Word choice in the original Greek text
suggests the ass Jesus rode Palm Sunday
into Jerusalem was wild. Yes, next
to fears that fickle crowds might yet one day
betray him, Jesus feared that fits and starts
from this donkey might thwart the prophecy
of how the messiah would gloriously
meet people's adulation. This upstart's
bucking ride would leave him in painful straits.
Thus, Jesus was a bit testy when he
at last reached the temple. Money changers
there had no chance. Jesus hit these strangers
with their blatant hypocrisy. When the
temper flared, in part, blame the burro's gaits.

Virgil Suarez

EXPULSION

How sorry is the capuchin monkey
or the ancient, solitary owl
up on its tree? Rubble and dust

glitter the way of the lovers,
mocked by their own shadows,
why so much guilt in their steps?

Flesh? They are displaced bodies,
after all, in search of the path home.
Call this rock a cave, this concave

a bed, this fallen branch or leaves
a pillow. What belongs in fire?
This word. If this is what paradise

is called, then it belongs to the fallen,
those in constant search in the world.
Absence is found only if you look back.

If you keep your eyes on the ground,
hold the trembling hand of your lover,
then the lights will shine in the distance.

Insect light? God's eyes, or a promise
of respite or a new journey. In either case,
you walk on, and move beyond here.

Susan Palwick

WAITING FOR PENTECOST

(Note: This essay was written during Advent 1999; the author was baptized as planned on the Feast of Pentecost, June 11, 2000.)

1. *Blessings*

When I tell friends, religious or otherwise, that I'm planning to be baptized in June, on the Feast of Pentecost, most of them give me a slightly puzzled look and then say sincerely, "Well, that's wonderful." I recognize the tone: it's the one I've used myself to congratulate people on taking up the Sousaphone, or deciding to bicycle around the world, or acquiring a spouse whose charm I simply can't fathom (*what* does she see in *him?*).

I can't blame my non-churchgoing friends for thinking this is all a little weird; so do I. After all, I never went to church as a child. Despite my increasingly urgent quest for faith, I never went to church at all until eighteen months ago, when I started attending a place that was very light on liturgy, and therefore nonthreatening. I liked the people there, but after a while, I realized that I was hungry for liturgy, for Scripture, for candles and vestments and stained-glass windows. So now, every Sunday, I go to St. Stephen's Episcopal Church in Reno, Nevada. Every Sunday I juggle the bulletin, the hymnal, and the Book of Common Prayer; every Sunday I stand and sing and kneel and recite the Nicene Creed, actions I never could have imagined myself performing two years ago. And every Sunday, when the baptized members of the congregation go to the altar rail to hold out their hands and receive Communion, I go there to receive a blessing from one of the priests. I go self-consciously; I'm grateful that St. Stephen's offers such blessings, that it includes the unbaptized in the procession to the altar rail, but as I kneel with my arms crossed in front of me — the signal to the priest to bless me, rather than offering me "the Body of Christ, the Bread of Heaven" — I'm also very aware that the gesture makes me look as if I'm hugging myself. This is a familiar posture; for most of my life, it's been the one I've adopted whenever I've been badly hurt, whenever I've felt as if my insides were about to spill out and I had to hold myself together to keep them in. Usually that hurt arose from the fact that I felt different from everyone else, which is exactly how I feel when I kneel at the altar rail, hugging myself while everyone else receives Communion.

After I'm baptized, I won't have to hug myself any more. After I'm baptized, I'll look just like everybody else, up there at the altar rail.

So why wait until Pentecost? That's the question I keep imagining my religious friends wanting to ask, the explanation I invent for their own puzzlement and hesitation when they congratulate me on my decision to be baptized. I could have been baptized at Easter or All Saints; as I write now, during Advent — the season of waiting, fittingly enough — I could still be baptized at

Christmas or on the Feast of the Epiphany. Why wait?

The simple, socially acceptable answer is that I want to be sure of my decision. A more personal answer is that I know myself well enough to know that if I have to wait for something, I won't take it for granted. But the real answer, both the simplest and the most personal, is that I love Pentecost.

Until this past May 23rd, I didn't even know what Pentecost was. When I went to church that day, one of the readings was from the Book of Acts, which comes immediately after the Gospels in the New Testament. Fifty days after Christ's resurrection, the apostles were all in one place, with many other people, when the Holy Spirit descended upon them in a mighty rushing wind, bestowing the gifts of prophecy, healing, and speaking in tongues. Whatever language anyone spoke at that gathering, everyone else could understand it. Pentecost, considered the beginning of the formal church, is a celebration of community, the reverse of the Tower of Babel. Three thousand people were baptized that day.

I'm a writer, and the most joyous and vivid moments of my life have been the moments of inspiration, the otherwise ordinary hours when I've gotten an idea for a book, a story, a poem. Those times always feel as if a mighty rushing wind has descended upon me and given me the ability to say things I wouldn't have been able to say otherwise. So when I heard the story of Pentecost for the first time at the age of thirty-eight, I knew that rushing wind. I knew, although I am hardly an apostle, a little of what it felt like to speak in tongues. The Holy Spirit's gift to me, all those years when I never went anywhere near a church, was the gift of writing, of language: how could I be baptized anytime other than Pentecost?

That's a good answer, a pleasing answer, and for several months I thought that was all there was to it. And then I read Kathleen Norris's description of Pentecost, in *Amazing Grace: A Vocabulary of Faith*, as "a vision of all of us coming together, bearing our different wounds, offering differing gifts. . . . Each of us speaking in the language we know, and being understood." Suddenly I was on my knees, hugging myself. I wasn't at the altar rail: I was in my living room, crying, doubled over in the old posture of pain. At that moment — which felt more like a sledgehammer than a rushing wind — I began to understand fully why I'm so hungry for the blessing Pentecost promises, and so willing to wait for it.

2. *Wounds*

Everyone's wounded: this isn't news, in the church or out of it, and I'm not about to claim special status. But I'm starting to believe that our greatest wounds are inseparable from our greatest gifts, that the two are inextricably entwined. As Jesus reminds us, "where your treasure is, there your heart will be also." In some ways, the Gospel words aren't that different from what my mother always told me when I was a child: "Susan, you have to stop wearing your heart on your sleeve, or you're going to get hurt."

My gifts — the things the mighty rushing wind brought me like Christmas presents, all year round — were the ability to feel deeply and the ability to talk about it, gifts of the heart and gifts of the tongue. I was an emotional kid, and one who talked a lot. But as much as I talked, all too often the people around me didn't seem to understand, didn't hear what I wanted them to hear. All too often they just stared at me, for all the world as if I were speaking in tongues. Reading Acts as an adult, I recognized that mighty rushing wind, but I recognized the scoffers, too. "All were amazed and perplexed, saying to one another, 'What does this mean?' But others sneered and said, 'They are filled with new wine.'"

Other kids sneered at me in junior high school when I actually laughed aloud at a funny book. Two girls in particular demanded to know why I was laughing, and when I showed them the passage, merely stared at me stonily. In college, I got a lecture from my roommate when I *didn't* laugh at some supposedly funny story about a traffic accident; I waited until everyone else had stopped laughing, and then asked, "But was anyone hurt?" My roommate, exasperated, told me I was too serious, that I didn't have a sense of humor.

I cite these two incidents not because they were especially painful, but because they were emblematic of patterns that have persisted into adulthood. On the one hand, I've learned that any visible or audible show of enthusiasm is suspect: my habit of exclaiming in joy at things that seem wonderful to me — meeting friends unexpectedly in a public place, discovering some new book by an author I love, finding a brand of tea I've been looking for forever, right there in the supermarket — consistently seems to mortify the people I'm with. I've become used to being told to calm down, to settle down, not to be so loud, not to get so worked up; various companions have actually stepped back from me, wrinkling their noses, when I acted too happy or excited.

On the one hand, then, I've received the clear message that being socially acceptable means being subdued. But on the other hand, much of the world seems to agree with my college roommate: I can't count the times I've been told I have no sense of humor, take things too seriously, need to lighten up. And indeed, I'm a dud at all too many parties and social occasions; I can't seem to get the hang of polite chit-chat. I keep wanting to have substantive conversations; I keep talking too much; I keep forgetting that when people say, "How are you?" most of them don't really want to know. It would be easier if one group of people found me too excitable and another found me too solemn, so that I could hang out with Group A when I felt serious and with Group B when I felt cheerful. It doesn't seem to work that way, though; it's more as if most people seem to think I'm both at once.

It would also be easier if my apparent inability to strike the proper tone were strictly a social handicap, but it's hampered me in professional situations, too. In graduate school, my professors kept telling me how naive I was because I talked about being emotionally moved by books. "Yes, that's how I used to respond to novels when I was an undergraduate," one eminent scholar told me during a seminar. At the department Christmas party a few months later, when I informed her that I was, in fact, thirty years old, she sniffed, turned on her heel and walked away, calling back over her shoulder, "Thirty going on nineteen, my dear!" A few years later, when I gave a bookstore reading after the publication of my first novel — surely an event about which I deserved to be excited — a woman in the audience walked up, sneered, looked me up and down, and said, "How old are you? Thirteen?"

Meanwhile, during my repeated forays into therapy (often prompted by my sense of social isolation), I've repeatedly been told that I'm not good enough at expressing my emotions, that I'm too intellectual, too verbal, too left-brained. If my speech often seems to be inappropriate for academic settings, it's routinely been dismissed as inauthentic in therapeutic ones. I'm too emotional in one place and too verbal in another. Too often, as I speak the wrong language in the wrong place, my meaning gets lost in translation.

I don't want to paint too grim a picture here; I've certainly been very successful at academic pursuits, and I have a cherished, if somewhat small, group of friends who value the same kind of conversation I do. I'm neither a professional disgrace nor a social pariah. But all too often, it's seemed as if the only place where my various qualities really all came together was on paper, where my combination of emotional intensity and verbal fluency helped me tell powerful stories. When you're by yourself in a room, writing, it's okay to cry, or laugh aloud: no one else is there to be embarrassed. And when you're writing, it helps — a lot — to be intense: intensity is the fuel that brings the story alive, that keeps you at your desk for the days or weeks or months you need to make the tale as vivid in the telling as it is in your head. Since childhood, I've sensed that my social awkwardness was the price I paid for the gifts I've been given. Here's Kathleen Norris again, in *The Cloister Walk*, talking about writers as "the necessary other:" "When artists discover as children that they have inappropriate responses to events around them, they also find, as they learn to trust those responses, that these oddities are what constitute their value to others."

I'm more grateful than I can possibly say that my work has been of value to others, that my first novel, *Flying in Place*, has been used in therapists' offices and court systems, that I've gotten praise from readers and from other writers. One woman wrote that she had been struggling with major depression, and that my book allowed her to cry for the first time in months. This means more to me than any number of successful cocktail-party conversations. So does the fact that on several occasions, I've been able to help depressed students: able to listen, able to help them get the help they needed. I may not be a great conversationalist at cocktail parties, but I can be pretty useful when people are hurting. I don't tell them to cheer up. I don't tell them it's just their imagination. I don't tell them they're being inappropriate or inauthentic: I tell them I know it hurts, that I know it can be hard even to get out of bed in the morning when you're depressed, that I know it can feel like the pain won't stop, ever, and that no one else understands or even really cares.

Been there, done that. Depression's been called the common cold of mental illness, and it thrives when people feel helpless, when they're put in no-win situations. Like being told that their joy is unacceptable, and so is their sorrow. Like being told that they're too emotional when they talk about their intellectual interests, and too intellectual when they talk about their emotions. It's hardly a surprise, then, that I've been struggling with chronic, low-level depression for most of my life. People kept telling me not to feel so much, or to feel differently. I didn't know how to do that, so all too often, I stopped feeling at all; instead, I watched the world through a thick, fuzzy barrier, as if I were wrapped in layers of cotton wool.

It wasn't a very good solution to the problem; it merely traded one kind of isolation for another, equally painful. And so in the early '90s, after years of various kinds of talk therapy, I finally decided to go ahead and try anti-depressants. I took Prozac for the next four years.

Prozac is a wonderful drug; it's saved the life of several friends. My case wasn't as serious as theirs, but Prozac helped me, too. It took the edge off, muted my intensity, made me more spontaneous in social situations and more tolerant of rejection. I didn't cry myself to sleep nearly as often, didn't feel the need to hug myself so much, and was more resilient in the face of stress. Prozac made it possible for me to perform several huge tasks that would have been much more difficult otherwise: finishing my PhD, spending three years on the national job market for college teaching jobs, moving across the country to take such a job, and, finally, learning to drive, a project that had terrified me for years. I got married on Prozac, bought a house on Prozac; I was a cheerful convert to meds.

I also, for the most part, stopped writing, and the writing I did was much more difficult. There were no ecstatic flights of fancy, no periods in which I became totally immersed in my work. My hard-won technical skills remained, and I slogged through my doctoral dissertation and a few short stories, but none of it was much fun, or particularly inspired. The Holy Spirit had stopped bringing me Christmas presents. When I was depressed, I'd looked at the outside world through cotton batting. On Prozac, I peered at my own creative process through the stuff. On Prozac, I also didn't care all that much; I was having a good time being more or less socially acceptable.

About a year and a half ago, the psychiatrist I was seeing suggested that I try going off Prozac, to see if I still needed it. He thought my new social skills might hold when I was off the meds, that four years might have permanently reset my emotional thermostat. (I also suspect that, as a good managed-care physician, he wanted to make sure that the expense of the drug was justified — a position with which, as a financially strapped new homeowner, I was sympathetic.) So I gradually decreased my dosage, until I was weaned completely.

In the past year, I've gotten more intense again. I've cried a lot more. I've seen people sneer at me when I got too excited about things, and watched them turn away in boredom when I went on a bit too long about something that mattered to me. I've also finished the first draft of my second novel and written two new stories and two personal essays. I haven't written this much — or, I think, this well — in years, certainly since long before my stint on medication.

During the hard times, the weepy times, I've debated going back on meds, but I'm scared of losing the writing again, and I always seem to snap out of my melancholy. I'm trying to be good about food and sleep and exercise, all of which are crucial to maintaining my mood. I stay in touch with friends, even or especially when I'm upset. I keep a journal of blessings, writing down all the good things, from the smallest to the most dramatic, that happen over the course of each day.

I've also started going to church, started formally thanking the Holy Spirit for the many gifts I've been given, started trying to live in relationship with a God who loves me however I happen to be feeling or speaking at the moment, a God who isn't going to tell me that I need to quiet down or lighten up. I'm trying to do an end-run around the cliche of the mentally ill artist who can't produce during times of health. This means that I have to redefine my ideas of health and sickness, and church is a good place to start. Listening to the huge emotional range of the Psalms, listening to Paul, in First Thessalonians, ad-monishing, "Do not quench the Spirit," I'm starting to think that maybe I haven't been sick all this time, but just different. Maybe the problem wasn't with me, but with a world that kept trying to force me into a mold I hadn't been designed to fit. I've started to suspect that most of the people who tried to silence me weren't doing so out of concern for me: they were doing it because I made them uncomfortable. And I welcome the insights that church, far more than therapy, has given me into certain kinds of ostracism.

Many of the non-Christians I know stereotype Christian churches — and perhaps especially Episcopal churches, long the province of the upper classes — as places where people go to fit in, to make a good impression on the neighbors while receiving facile assurances of God's love. But even the most cursory reading of the New Testament refutes the notion that Christianity is about either conformity or comfort. Jesus was a radical: he came to turn the existing social order on its head, and the existing social order, in self-defense, ensured that he died in agony. This is an appalling story, even for people who believe in the resurrection. The message isn't about reassurance: it's about life, about paradox and messiness, about the fact that blessings and wounds inevitably come together, yin and yang, the matched set of incarnation. If our gifts set us apart from others, we will probably wind up being wounded, and the only way to redeem our wounds is to transform them — using the same gifts that ensured our wounding in the first place — into something other people can use, into blessings. No one can call any of this easy. The Kingdom of God is not a cocktail party.

It's not a place for finger-pointing, either, as Jesus kept so pointedly re-minding his followers. The church tells me to forgive the people who've hurt me. I still find that difficult, and perhaps I always will, but the alternative is to shut them out the same way I've been shut out, to become the very thing that has wounded me. Every day now, sometimes twice a day, I pray the words of St. Francis, asking that I may seek not so much to be understood as to under-stand. The phrase makes me wince each time I repeat it. Trying to understand the people who have belittled me, I wonder if perhaps they were afraid, or simply clumsy and careless, as I have been so often. I try to be compassionate towards them. It doesn't always work.

Early on in my Prozac days, when my head had cleared enough for me to get some perspective on the patterns I've been writing about here, I tried to talk to my therapist about the fact that I'd so often been punished for being happy. I'd been going to this therapist for eight years; she knew me well, had seen me through a lot, and had agreed with me when I railed about the pain and injustice of various family problems. She was someone I trusted. She admired my intelligence and creativity, and had always given me emphatic permission to air my more negative feelings. But when I asked her, "Why did all those people try to smother my joy? How could they do that? It's like they were trying to kill my soul," she just rolled her eyes.

"No they weren't," she said briskly. "They were trying to teach you to be more self-contained, and you still need to work on that."

I think I went into shock when she said that; I know I didn't argue with her. I dutifully worked on being more self-contained. It was a long time before I acknowledged how much it hurt that someone who knew me so well had treated me like radioactive waste. Now, wondering if the message I heard is the one she wanted me to hear, I struggle for a forgiveness which is the opposite of self-containment. Forgiveness moves outward, like the hands of people reaching for Communion.

Hugging myself at the altar rail at St. Stephen's is a profoundly paradoxical gesture: at once my personal posture of self-comfort and my communal request for clerical comfort, the way I protect myself from the pain of difference and the way I maintain my difference from the people kneeling on either side of me. If I keep the toxic stuff in, this gesture says, they won't cast me out; but at the same time, my stubborn waiting is my way of testing that it's safe for me to stand out in church, that I don't need to do exactly what everyone else does. When I begin to take Communion, I want it to be for the right reasons, because I'm reaching for redemption and not for decorum. When I become more like everyone else in church, a member of Christ's body, I will also be affirming my unlikeness, my willingness — in fear and trembling and considerable skepticism — to be Christ's sore thumb.

This is scary business. One of our priests tells me that most of the people who ask for blessings at the altar rail are children. That's fitting, she says gently, because I'm a child in the church, and I need to be as open and willing to learn as a child. I'm working at it, but I suspect that even after my adoption into the family, I'll still fear being sent away for saying the wrong thing. And so I'm waiting for Pentecost, the Feast of All Tongues, when I can speak in the language I know, and be understood.

3. *Promises*

At Pentecost, no one will tell me that I'm inappropriate or inauthentic. At Pentecost, no one will tell me to quiet down or to lighten up. That's the promise that made me cry, when I read Norris's description.

It's metaphorical, of course. I know that. I'm waiting now for a particular day on the calendar, June 11th of the year 2000, when a priest will pour water over my forehead and then annoint me with chrism, when I and others will promise to follow Christ. Probably, no one will even really hear us say the words, because if my own baptism is anything like the others I've witnessed, there are going to be a lot of very unhappy, very loud babies in church that day. And we'll let them cry, and we'll baptize them anyway, because nobody would dream of demanding that infants be self-contained.

Knowing me, I'll cry too, when the priest pours the water on my forehead (unless I get a fit of the giggles instead, which would be much worse), but I highly doubt that anyone will sneer at me. I'll go back to my pew, where I'll juggle the bulletin and the hymnal and the Book of Common Prayer, and afterwards there will be coffee and cake, and then I'll go home, and life will go on pretty much as usual.

And I'll keep waiting for Pentecost, because it's not just one day on a calendar. Just as the Kingdom of God permeates the world, is everywhere in daily life if only you know how to see it, so all the church seasons are contained in each moment, too, all of it contained in God who contains all times, who is all times. Each moment is Advent when we wait, and Christmas when hope arrives incarnate in the world; Easter when hope arises from its own tomb, and Pentecost when we are filled with the gifts of the spirit, with the gift of understanding and being understood, even by the sneerers.

This is, perhaps, the part of the story I like best, the part that fills me with (no doubt terribly unchristian) glee: the conversion of the mockers, who are "cut to the heart" by Peter's speech. The apostles aren't filled with new wine, he tells the skeptics: they're filled with the Holy Spirit. And the skeptics repent, and are baptized themselves. I can't help but see this as a vindication of the socially unacceptable, Pentecost as revenge of the nerds. When I imagine that gathering, I see my college roommate standing there, sneering, and next to her the condescending professor from graduate school, and my therapist, and all the mean kids in junior high school, and all the people who ever told me to quiet down, to lighten up. And I see their eyes becoming as big as saucers when they finally get it, when they finally understand what's being said to them. The Holy Spirit's for them, too. It's for anyone who'll accept it, anyone who'll listen, anyone who'll open up. You don't have to wear stylish clothing, or know the latest jokes, or be on the right guest list.

This vision will never happen in any literal sense, of course. But I hope— and I hope I'm being forgiving when I hope it—that someday my mockers will stop sneering and start listening, to others and to themselves. I hope that someday they'll start learning to trust the inappropriate, as I'm learning to trust it. That's the promise of Pentecost, and it's worth the wait.

William F. Bell

CONVERSION

Last night when the temperature fell
And the wind changed altogether,
I felt the shock of a parallel
Change in my own weather.

Notions I could no longer brook
Collapsed in the night and were gone,
Making space for a new outlook
To come in the cold dawn.

No wonder that I felt queasy
Like a voyager fresh to the sea,
For the change would not be easy,
However needful for me.

Some, I know, find nothing strange
When their lives take on a new shape;
They speed like runners to greet the change
And charge against the tape,

But I am a jogger, timid and slow,
And with second thoughts I pause,
Afraid of the self I do not know
And clutching the self I was.

Walt McDonald

MAY ALL OF OUR BABIES HAVE ANGELS

Killing takes timing, leading a deer
to steel. Hold the string bow taut
and let go, knowing an arrow goes fast
till it falls or something blunt stops it,

even a body softer than barbs.
We never aim into shadows: steel flies
wherever we point, even if fingers slip.
May all of our babies have angels.

If our son's out of work, some year,
he's a target. Or maybe he's driving home
and a drunk runs a red light.
Assume he's happy for decades

and life is a romp through the woods.
DNA like a dart may flip cancer
steel-tipped and slicing through shadows,
not wobbling, and razor sharp.

Nancy Tupper Ling

A LITTLE FAITH

To a six-month old
Mommy is God.
Her faith's secure,
simple, not blind.
She knows her creator,
falling asleep to her
pulsating heartbeat,
tummy rumbles
from wombside.

From birth she worships her,
trusting solid arms
to enfold her, catch her
pre-fall. Any stray smiles,
signs of her existence,
send her tiny body
gleefully convulsing.
And should her saviour
leave a room, she'll
weep uncontrollably,

believing her dead.

Leo Luke Marcello

OUR LADY OF THE ISLANDS

The city is preparing for the coming day, the Day of the Dead. Inside the old cathedral in downtown San Antonio, pilgrims are praying, readying themselves for the feast. Flags are raised. The church is filled with flowers and burning candles. In front of the main altar is the smaller, temporary altar loaded with flowers and food and photographs of the dead. Here and there a person shuffles forward to place a lighted candle. Someone else gets up from a pew, genuflects, and leaves quietly.

I pray for a while, aware of the comings and goings of people around me. The church is not full. I can only imagine the crowd that will fill it the next day, the actual Day of the Dead, when processions will take the flags and statues out of the church, through the front door and down the street along the river. I will not be in the city for the festivities, but I try to imagine what it will be like among the crowd, joyful and mournful, music in the air, incense, bells ringing against the blue sky.

I have been praying for quite a while in the church before I see the strange figure far back in the recesses behind the main altar. She is tall, even taller because of the base upon which she stands, a strange madonna and child. She stares out over the church like a giant stone Buddha, a headpiece like a collar, a huge cowl, and drapery hanging down from her, past her feet, past pedestal, hanging down over the candles before her but not catching their flames. In her arms the child leans. I cannot see them clearly from this distance, so I make my way up the aisle.

As I approach, she becomes more enigmatic, her face blank as the Buddha's but with eyes open. She stares beyond us all toward the horizon. The child leans, balanced only in air. If it were a real child, it would fall, but the weight of the wood out of which it is carved depends upon the fibers of the tree out of which it had been carved. It leans, a young prince, a king-to-be, while the mother stands still for centuries.

Her red damask robe bears the years well. The gold threads maintain their stitches. The collar-crown rests upon her head. For centuries, her subjects have cared for her finery. She might as easily have been a Spanish queen as the queen of heaven. I wonder if her clothes have been cleaned periodically. Is she ever stripped of this material? The wood of her face seems stone, the peacefulness of stone never to wear away, but to endure.

I gaze upon her. I cannot gaze enough upon her.

Finally, I go next door into the cathedral shop to inquire. "Who is the madonna?" There are no prayer cards for her, no statues, cheap or otherwise, of this particular image. But a woman working in the shop goes into the back to ask for me. The answer comes back: *"Nuestra Senora de Candelaria.* She came with the first settlers," the woman says.

A customer standing next to me turns and asks, "Are you a descendant?" The woman's eyes are dark. They twinkle with eager beads of light.

"No," I answer and just as suddenly regret that I am not, for what answer might

I have received had I claimed being of that line?

The woman smiles and buys her candle and prayer cards and goes away.

I return to the cathedral and to Our Lady of the Islands, and I kneel there for some immeasurable time. She stares beyond me, over my head. The early settlers had brought her from the Canary Islands. She steered their ocean voyage into this safe place. She has seen things that she does not care to speak. She does not smile. She does not weep.

She is not the pietà they would later invoke. She is the infinite hope of pilgrims, the wood that does not crack. She remains with them. She reminds them without words. She is here so long as her robes do not catch flames from the candles below, so long as the pilgrims bear her through the streets on their shoulders on such holy days, over the waters of their journeys, in the vessels over land and sea, even into the cold air of their annual feast.

I say an Amen and walk back to my hotel. It happens that today the President and his wife are going to visit the Alamo. I have been thinking for some years now that I might one day meet them. It happens that they have among their best friends one of my best friends. This is not a fact that I have mentioned to many people. Most likely I will never meet the President and his wife. We will probably never sit at the same table with our mutual friend. Life is too short for everything to happen, and there are regrets and blessings in this shortness.

But as I am approaching my hotel, the forces of security ward me away. I cannot take the familiar street back to the hotel. I am forced to take another street. Walking against the crowd, I make my way back through the shadowy street of the otherwise bright blue morning. The weather has turned, and I welcome the cold wind. Back in Louisiana I know that the cemeteries are filled with the traditional orange and yellow and white chrysanthemums, that the white tombs have been whitewashed anew, that the shrubs have been trimmed, the grass cut, the roads edged. But I am walking through a street in San Antonio, walking against the flow of pedestrians seeking the Presidential motorcade. No doubt, I appear a suspicious character, though I am well dressed and on my way back to a poetry reading at the hotel.

Suddenly I find myself on the sidewalk in front of my hotel, and just at that very moment, the Presidential motorcade passes. The President waves. Beside him the First Lady turns her head to wave to the opposite side of the street. The car is gone in an instant.

I go into the hotel thinking of their hands waving, thinking of the eyes of the madonna, the almost stone-face of the Buddha. Tomorrow the people of San Antonio will carry their procession through the streets. The Day of the Dead will have another day. In another year the faces of the procession will have changed again. I will not be in San Antonio next year on this day. The President and the First Lady have seen the Alamo. If they ever return, it will probably not be on this day.

But Our Lady of the Islands will still be standing within the cathedral walls. She will be wearing her red damask robes and large collar-crown. Her child will still be balanced in her arms. Her eyes will continue to stare out over the horizon. She will be standing there as long as there are people to light candles before her, so long as she does not catch flames from their candles. She will be staring beyond us, all of us, descendants and not descendants, and it will not matter if we are from the Canary Islands or Louisiana. We can count on that gaze even more than we can count on being here ever again.

Stella Nesanovich

OUT OF THE COURT OF MY FATHER

The medieval mystic, Mechthild of Magdeburg, shortly after her move to the Beguinage, 1230

Out of the court of my father,
his royal house, to live amid cesspools
and lice. Alms my Beguine sisters offer,
servants to beggars in tattered shirts,
barren maidens, pox-ridden fowlers,
and children who hunger for soup.
For God's love I moved to this town,
fled home to witness ailments
only He can heal. Daily we chant,
pray for bishop Norbert and the poor.
Yet we reside with stench and clamor—
where my Lord also dwells, I remember.

In this upheaval Spirit comes again.
Such force enters my heart then that I can
no longer yield to complaint but see
with eyes of my soul the presence of Jesus
in His creatures, all within the Godhead
as fish within vast oceans. What sweetness
and heavenly wisdom greet me, visions
of Christ's manhood and divinity!
Revelations as none my brain could know
prove gracious lessons of gentle Love,
a lady who shoulders my woes, bathes
my brow when fevered, and teaches:
if a pure wick of humility burns,
a candle's flame will shine far.

Stella Nesanovich

THE SOUL AND THE SENSES: A DIALOGUE

The medieval mystic, Mechthild of Magdeburg, alone, 1235

Soul

From that vision I awakened
chaste as the sacrificial lamb,
my mate in swooning sweet accord
as lovers on their wedding couch.
Pleasures like honey from a comb
no corporal tongue has known,
spirit tingling with dripping dew,
juice of grace and Paradise.

Body

We perish in such boundlessness.
Senses, on guard! Hasten to retreat!

Soul

Ah, body, so armed against me
with all nature's weaponry.
Loose your mail of Saxon silver,
ungird your sheath, so love may kiss
your breasts. Fire draws us.
Like warmth of husband's caress,
our redeemer of soul and sense.

Body

Do not hasten, Lady Soul,
the flame of love devours.
The scalding blade of death
this sacrifice does bode.

Soul

But such demise means life yet.
Recall the grain of wheat must die,
so in love's sweet chamber
as self does sink, Christ will rise.
Dance, oh heart, double round.

Stella Nesanovich

DAS FLIEßENDE LICHT DER GOTTHEIT: A VISION SEQUENCE

The medieval mystic, Mechthild of Magdeburg, alone, 1245

A vision at first most horrid: darkness clamping the valley.
Where once figs and grapes filled every hill
so far as human eye can witness, I saw only graves.
Then armies waged war with great iron forks and spears
here in Saxon glens. For each soul they fought
before an oven where Lucifer swallowed many.
Sodomites slithered down his throat to live in his belly.
Eternal death followed soldiers who pillaged.
Thieves, strung up by their feet, served as beacons,
but the damned saw nothing, for Satan beguiled
with clever words: "I am cocky as a fly who lands
on all." Then I heard our Lord above the din:
"They compassed me about like bees;
they blazed like fire among thorns."

I could not speak until Love flowed to greet me.
Voices raised in praise chanted of gardens,
streams of milk and holy ground. Everywhere
hearts of golden hue pulsed through firmaments
as rain of stars and meteors. Then rose
great numbers of souls free from purgatory,
their robes white with bliss. God's brass-filled voice
spoke again: "I am a flowing spring of love
no devil may dam with idle thoughts."
Zithers and harps sounded for dancers
to enter and circle a meadow in garlands
of virtues, consciences pure. I prayed
to teach the sweet taste of goodness,
to write of our Savior's pleasurable touch.

Saw I next a veil like the hunger cloth
that hangs before the altar during Lent,
symbol of our penance, yet this most resembled
a membrane of an egg, the thin shutter
between earth and heaven. Down the middle
lay stripes of gold bordered with precious stones

and woods, bolts Adam fastened to pierce Jesus
that He might loose them by His rising.
Four beams shot forth to strike the veil, the Gospels
numbing the tongues of those already deaf,
light for the path of God's Word.

Now my German falters, for the veil opened
to show forth many doors with different rewards
for virgins, widows, and faithful married couples.
Hell's mouth gaped, but souls escaped
through Christ's grace. They streamed to paradise,
where a voice proclaimed their coming:
"Receive, Lord, your brides, and meet them with roses
for diligence brought them to this blessed end."

In a damp cell, upon my knees I stayed.
My sisters returning, my senses having failed,
I worshipped in silence.

Stella Nesanovich

THE UNMOORED SOUL

The medieval mystic, Mechthild of Magdeburg, leaving the Beguinage of
Saint Agnes, 1269

Slapped by rage, scourged by poverty,
I am crowned with trials, as our sweet Lord:
spat upon, cast out, an unmoored soul
unsafe from calumny, men of stony core
who close their ears to words the Spirit sows.
Stinking goats, they convert temples
into squalid barns, would flay me.

I did not wish for fame, as Satan claims.
The golden tongue of Wisdom spoke—I obeyed.
Meister Heinrich urged record of those thoughts,
himself the circuit of my book, which now he hides,
charging I write as man, not as woman should.

My sisters shut their doors. I hear murmurs.
Gudrun says preaching will bring interdict
on my sheep. What weight the crosier carries!
Some call me heretic. Unvowed to God,
I have no home. Dark as an ocean storm,
the desert beckons, "Come, nomad."

In dreams a cloistered nun in white wimple
calls me to her garden where sweet flowers
blossom despite spiny, thin-leafed weeds.
How lovely God's dwelling place! My soul
recalls the warmth of home and hopes for health,
balm for aging eyes, blessings and chanting
of holy hours, peace in the courts of my Lord.

Kathryn Thompson Presley

RITES OF PASSAGE

The green bathing suit first captivated our family in the 60's. It was an ugly, one-pieced jersey affair which would become the centerpiece of family rituals. Aunt Rosie and Uncle Franklin had recently built a new home overlooking Wild Horse Creek, complete with swimming pool, barbecue pit and arrangements for comfortably feeding and sleeping a crowd! I don't think anyone envied Franklin and Rosie their new wealth, certainly no one who knew how hard they had worked during the depression to buy and hold on to the few rocky acres that became their home place for sixty years. Aunt Rosie had worked part time at the library in Chickasaw Springs while driving over to Ada to finish her teaching certificate. Then she taught the "little room" (grades one through four) at Wild Horse School. Uncle Franklin worked at a succession of jobs in town: feed store clerk, hardware clerk, and finally postal clerk which he remained until his retirement. They had no children, lived frugally and had begun to prosper, even before "wildcatters" discovered their dry little farm floated on a rich pool of oil. Rosie was my mother, Lily's, older sister and there was a younger girl, Daisy, and one boy whom they called "Bud." The McClure family took a lot of good natured teasing for naming their red headed, freckled faced children after flowers. But, in their hardscrabble lives, those children were a source of joy and beauty.

Rosie and Franklin had no children, a major disappointment to them both, but they "adopted" all of us nephews and nieces along with every child out at Wild Horse Creek. After our grandparents died, Aunt Rosie and Uncle Franklin quietly took their places and all our holidays, every summer vacation included a trip to their "homeplace" out at Wild Horse Creek. When no nieces or nephews were around, they took in all the children of their community. No one ever knew for sure how many young people had their college tuition paid by my aunt and uncle.

Our first visit to their new house was in 1962 and I had failed to bring a bathing suit. Aunt Rosie offered one but it was scaled to her tiny body and I was well on my way to six feet by then. My sister, Eileen offered one of hers, but she was far too buxom. Undaunted, Aunt Rosie dashed in to town and found one just my size at the local five and dime. It was not at all flattering, but it would do. We played water tag, floated on an old air mattress, and practiced our diving. It was a golden summer and we reluctantly said good-bye to Uncle Franklin and Aunt Rosie in August, just before the new school term began. By then, the green bathing suit had turned a ghastly shade of chartreuse in the chlorine and hot Oklahoma sun, and stretched so that I had to pin it in place with safety pins. There was a lot of heckling about my appearance in the old thing, so I dumped it, with some relief, in the laundry room trash before leaving.

We never knew who retrieved it, but always suspected Uncle Franklin. That Christmas I opened an elaborately wrapped package from Oklahoma and found the neatly laundered, still hideous bathing suit. We had a good laugh, and I carried it with me to an "after Christmas" weekend celebration at Wild Horse. When we left for home, the bathing suit reposed in a tinsel box far back under the wilting Christmas tree.

It resurfaced at my graduation party the following year. A beautiful, three tiered cake was delivered the afternoon before the party. That night, when I tried to cut the cake, it was only frosting over pasteboard and inside, you guessed it, lay the old green bathing suit.

Obviously, a family tradition was evolving. Over the next thirty years, we included other nieces, nephews, aunts and uncles in the fun. Uncle Bud found the green monstrosity in the glove compartment of his new car—a birthday surprise from Aunt Rosie and Uncle Franklin. Over the years, Aunt Rosie found the suit in a variety of places: inside the podium where she had taught Sunday School for decades, in her bread box, wrapped in freezer paper in her freezer, dangling from the dining room chandelier and beneath the make-up drawer in her overnight case.

I found it in the top drawer of my desk at my first teaching job. It appeared in my sister's suitcase when she was at the hospital having her third baby. Our cousin, Amy-Ruth, found it gift wrapped among her wedding presents, and cousin Taylor found it in his briefcase when he arrived at court to argue his first case.

Over the decades, that old green suit became a part of every family gathering, and most of our rites of passage. When my cousin Rosetta's husband, Joshua, was promoted and transferred to Atlanta, they found the green bathing suit hanging on the front door of their white colonial mansion. We never knew how Rosie did that— or even if it was Rosie's work? Part of the fun was, we could never be sure who had the bathing suit at a given moment in time. I do know that just before Christmas of 1982, aunt Rosie received the suit, by federal express, in a plastic baggie, buried in a large can of caramel corn. I know, because I was there when she found it.

By now, the third generation was eagerly participating; in fact, my niece, Kathy, bravest of the lot, wore the thing to a midnight swim party given for her graduation class. With appropriate safety pins and tucks, and in the moonlight, the suit looked almost glamorous. By day, however, it showed its advancing age, just like the rest of us.

It seems to me that one day we were all young, and the next we were old—or at least middle aged. Aunt Rosie began to wear her fading ginger hair in a bun, just as grandma had done. Uncle Franklin seemed to shrink and grow quieter every year. When, one October night, he died in his sleep at the age of 87, he left a larger hole in our lives than we would ever have imagined! Aunt Rosie looked very small and forlorn when we left her alone in that big house after the services. We urged her to move to the city near us, or at least visit us, but she stayed on alone. The farm had been leased out years before and she had a faithful housekeeper and gardener, husband and wife, who had become a part of our family. Rosie took to wearing Franklin's old plaid flannel shirts, and kept his pipe waiting near his easy chair. Though sadder and wiser, we were busily launching children and our lives went on, pretty much the same.

The Thanksgiving after Franklin died, our entire clan descended on Rosie bearing smoked turkeys and hams, home baked pies and cakes. Aunt Rosie made her famous rolls and, except for the empty chair at the head of the table, it was almost like every Thanksgiving of our lives, especially when my husband carved the turkey and found the green bathing suit, in its familiar plastic bag, stuffed in the cavity.

For Christmas that year, we got aunt Rosie to join us, somewhat reluctantly, at a ski resort near Vail. One day, she rode the ski lift up to watch us and our children (with two grandchildren now) learning to ski. After that, she sat by the fire in the lodge and elicited their life stories from every one she met. Rosie was like that. And when we opened gifts on Christmas morning, Eileen's youngest grandchild, Rebekah, found an old green bathing suit wrapped around her Teddy bear.

The suit went into hiding for a while after that. Rebekah's mother, Carrie, is an absent minded soul, a dear thing but a procrastinator. And, I think, she had difficulty coming up with original ideas for transmitting the suit. We had done it all by then. But not quite.

My husband, Wes, retired in 1995 and our wild Scots Irish clan gathered to honor him with a reception. Everyone came except Eileen and her middle daughter who was giving birth to triplets, Doug, Drew, and Roy Lee, in San Diego. My husband is a shy, quiet soul, more comfortable with his books than with people. So it seemed incongruous when the caterer showed up with a gargantuan, multi-tiered cake. Midway through the dinner, our granddaughter, Rachel, sprang out of the cake—wearing the green bathing suit. She made haste to change costumes for the suit was, by now, quite fragile.

After that, the old bathing suit went underground again and was almost forgotten in our concern for aunt Rosie's health. She had a series of heart attacks that summer, and by October, around-the-clock nurses were required. There were several long stays at Baptist Memorial Hospital in Oklahoma City. They did not feel she could tolerate heart surgery, so Wes and I spent a lot of time on the farm with her that year. It was during the first snow of the season that she "set sail for Glory." We had given her nurse the night off, so aunt Rosie stayed up later than usual, happy as a child as she watched snow falling outside her window. We had shared her favorite potato soup at a table in her sitting room, listening to the Gaithers and remembering other winter nights.

"I don't know why I was chosen," she whispered, her old face luminous with joy. "Why was I given so much happiness, such a home, such a family?"

She clasped my hand affectionately, and all the hard work, the disappointments, sorrows were swallowed up in joy. I had been reading one of Dr. Scott Peck's books dealing with the stages of grief: denial, anger, negotiation, depression, acceptance. He said they applied, not only to grieving for death, but for all the traumas of life. Few people ever reach acceptance, but watching my Aunt Rosie on that snowy evening, I knew she was one of the fortunate few.

When I checked on her shortly after midnight, she was still and cold—the doctor said she died shortly after I kissed her goodnight. All of us were unprepared for the powerful sense of loss. She was eight-six; hers was a life well-lived, and our lives were busy and full, but she had been a major part of our existence for so long—especially Eileen's and mine. The familiar last rituals helped for a time; she had paid for her funeral and planned the service long before. But there were motel rooms to reserve, meals to supervise. The outpouring of food, flowers and affection nearly overwhelmed us. By the time we assembled in the little chapel to pay our last respects, we were all bordering on exhaustion.

"I'll fly away, oh glory, I'll fly away," the sweet young voice seemed to drift down to us from somewhere up behind the baptistry. It might have been aunt Rosie's voice, describing her homeward journey. The young country preacher gave a brief eulogy, summarizing aunt Rosie's long, rich life in only a few sentences, but his conclusion stayed with me. "Miss Rosie was blessed of God and generously shared her blessings with a host of nieces, nephews, neighbors, and friends." Most of us were crowded into the little chapel that day and after the town preacher gave a brief message, we stood to sing "Amazing Grace," a capella. There were few dry eyes as we filed past the flower bedecked casket. Whispering our goodbyes to our aunt, Eileen and I were both gripped simultaneously by powerful emotion. Burying our faces in lace handkerchiefs, we leaned heavily on our husbands who helped us out into the bright sunshine. The congregation wept in sympathy for our sorrow; but family members understood the real nature of our emotion as they filed past Rosie's casket. There, just visible amid the tulle, lace, and roses, trailed a faded strap of the old green bathing suit, headed at last for its final resting place.

Chris Ellery

BASIC ANATOMY OF THE CHEST

In the cadaver room
I held a heart
the size of a football.
It was stiff with formaldehyde,
very, very cold,
and motionless.

How much must a man have to love
to grow a heart so big?

Oh, I know what you are thinking:
it was obesity and disease
that swelled it into silence.
Doubtless you have read the texts
on myocardial infarction,
congestive heart failure. There have been studies,
refereed, in famous journals
on congenital afflictions.

But I am thinking of a man
who sat on sunset bluffs alone
and lacked a priest's or poet's words
to tell his wonder,
who fed cats in lieu of wife and child
to hold and whisper to,
who watched the news
on Christmas Eve
and lacked the notes to sing
or chords to strum away
the thick sorrow gathering
under his sternum.
Might not sentiment, unexpressed,
stuff a heart to bursting?

Note well the valves
and chambers of this organ,
cut from the body that encased it.
Read the map-like veins
and arteries beneath the pericardium.
See how the bloodless aorta gapes
like a plastic mouth,
as though to whisper, sing, or kiss.

Chris Ellery

THE STORY PRAYS FOR THE POET

A child will pray for in-line skates
with wheels as free as wind, fabulous
as the bean-stalk truth of storybooks.

The liar will pray for a license, for a pigeon
fat as birds under bridges, as judges
who stand on disaster.

Disasters pray for a surgeon, a surgeon
for the clean incision, for that wriggling
little beast the heart, cupped in latex hands.

A virgin prays to the hands nailed to a crucifix.
The lunatic watching her prays to himself, knowing
God is madder than he is.

The artist invokes the light, pigment
to catch the light, quick as the tongue
of a lizard.

The lizard prays for dragonflies, dragonflies
for swamps. The swamp prays for water, water
for myths as true as maidens.

The myth prays for the maiden, the maiden
for a child, a story to tell the child.
The story prays for the poet.

John McKernan

IN WILLIAM BLAKE'S 1799 PEN &

Tempera painting on paper "The Virgin

Hushing the Young Baptist Who Approaches

The Sleeping Infant" A wide-eyed wild

Baby John   (Nude like he's just crawled out

Of some creek) With a Monarch butterfly

In his right palm   Slips through the door

To Mary's left with its Capuan background

Tower of Babel Etna Pompeii Stands still

At Mary's single finger stop-sign hand &

Bends his head to stare at cousin Jesse

Sleeping like a cloud on folds of white cloth

Her silence coaxing John to quiet   Hushed

As an alphabet in memory She knows   She

Knows her child needs his sleep His Sleep

John McKernan

THE NEW KID WITH THE ARAMAIC ACCENT

From Bethlehem is always scribbling Hebrew letters
In the dust with his kitten on the edge of town

He's forever playing with those toys from Egypt
The whistling top with its four-color corners
The wood ball he spins on his index finger

His dad's a roofer   Has lots of Roman clients
Makes intricate chairs   Spends most of his time
Tinkering   He loves to build new hammers
And carve wood knots into sharp nails / dowels

That's his mother   Standing in moonlight   Looks
Like she's crying again   Keeps talking about men
With gifts speaking incredible languages
How she told them her dream of the snake
Turning into a dove   No one understood one word

Donald Carlson

INTROIBO AD ALTARE DEI

Four words alone redeem the day;
The void grows pregnant when they're said:
Introibo ad altare Dei.

When my feet begin to stray
And *taedium vitae* dogs my tread,
Four words alone redeem the day.

Nine syllables that will allay
The muddle that confounds my head
Are *Introibo ad altare Dei.*

No earthly magic can defray
Terror of terminal dread.
Four words alone redeem the day.

No other mantra I can say
Promises angelic bread
But *Introibo ad altare Dei.*

When I become too numb to pray
And the Spirit's flame seems dead,
Four words alone redeem the day:
Introibo ad altare Dei.

CONSECRATION

hallowed hands hold bread
white moon crests snowy mountain
here all worlds buckle

John Wolf

EVEN SO

Every day brought offerings of iron and gold.
You can see in these rust-stained hands
the choices I made, what I've kept and sold
for nothing, or nearly so, and what now stands,
caught in the doorsill between light and dark,
not able to step out, not willing to stay in.
And so I seek forgiveness and love that arc
out over the night sky, and black clouds thin
in their tenderness, their arms wanting more
than ordinary hearts could bear or even know.
Tell me, tell me there's a place for the poor,
the pale of heart, where sacred lovers go,
where grace encircles all that grace can find,
the lost, the dire, and even so the blind.

Anne Higgins

CHARLESTON WINTER

I sit on the bed above the chimneys.
Palmetto trees,
willows, live oaks,
disappear into the candlelight
blue in the solstice light,
air still warm,
red camellias blooming in the garden below.

I sit on the bed,
thinking sunset
over the mountain
in Maryland,
 deer leaping in the empty battlefield,
grey deer with tree bark
in snow scattered grey grass.

I sit on the bed,
thinking Thomas Merton
walking Kentucky woods
in blue December light
twenty years ago
checking on trees he planted
in anguish,
 loblolly pines
grown tall and graceful,
bending in the sharp
December wind,
taller still
twenty years later,
 trees
he planted in anguish.

I sit on the bed,
checking on trees I planted...
Pink crab apple trees
twenty years ago...
Palmettos tonight.

Anne Higgins

TALENTS

What does it mean to enter into your Master's joy?
Come. He's back,
who has new things to do,
who has yet more to say.

And what did I do while he was away?
So long away. What did I do?

What is joy made of?
Are its walls water
or slick black rock?

Some will go there
in spite of everything.
The wet wings of the grey dusky swift
in Argentina,
up in the highest place
where Argentina meets Peru,
the fine wings fly through the waterfall,
fly to its thinnest fabric and fly through it,
groping, clumsy and wet,
up the dark slick rock
and into the slice of rock
to the nest.

Come—enter your master's joy.
The master of reins, the God of rain,
the raining God, the reigning God calls
Come,
enter into your master's joy,
into the scandalizing center of it.
My wings fly through the forgiving wall of water.
My clumsy, wet, yearning body
clambers up to it,
to the small crevice,
to the nest.

Anne Higgins

SAYING THE ROSARY

I used to say it on St. Paul Street
In bed, to go to sleep,
That small brown rosary
From the souvenir store at the catacombs in Rome...
Cecilia lying on her side, her hair swept back, the slice in her neck..
How I used to fall asleep saying it, lying on that sofa bed in the octagonal
living room,
In my light night gown,
With the traffic pouring by outside,
And the window fan on,
In the heat of the summer night,
Praying to be spared from robbers
And rapists,
Praying for sleep
To pull me quickly and safely to the morning.
And he filled me with a song I never sang,
A rose I never saw,
Waves too distant for birds.

FIXING THE LOCK

Lock broken after years of use.
Removed from the wrench of the door
Slim, tarnished as a cigarette box
brass, flat, it sat in the wood
like a coin in the eye of the dead.
Unscrewed from its long residence,
entirely slipping out into hand
like a secret passageway opening
smooth, silent, dust in the lubrication.
Six small screws loosened, removed,
clotted with timedust, oil, doordust.
Brass box opens, shows
springs, clips, buds of metal
oilblack, sandgrime,
now to the blind repair,
uncertain reassemblage.

Anne Higgins

STORM LIGHTENING, CHARLESTON

Juice rises in straw like a bad wire,
current flashing from nave to buttress,
unseemly, fallowed by whacking thunder
harpy's hammer against
garbage galvanized,
an old man in the alley on New Year's eve,
smashing his kitchen pot,
his household hammer.
Death in the grass,
in the sidewise rain,
birds fleeing into the
side turned leaves,
all their palms up.

Pennylyn Dykstra-Pruim

REDEFINING SUCCESS

One spring Mom had this great idea. Gramma should leave the chilly drabness of The Windy City and join my snowbird parents for a brief stay in sunny Florida. At the time, I was well on my way to a noble if not lucrative academic career, by attending graduate school on the sunnier but colder side of Lake Michigan. So when Mom suggested that I might accompany Gramma to Boynton Beach, Florida, I was interested. After all, March is generally a chilly month in Madison, Wisconsin. We keep the mittens and mufflers in our coat pockets until at least April. Indeed, spring break in Florida sounded pretty good, but I was also a bit worried. I was counting on studying my way through spring break in order to catch up or get ahead, depending on which I needed most when the time rolled around. And I had this husband. The relationship was going pretty well, but who knows what a week away would do? A profound philosophical question lingered in my mind. Which of the following is really true: "Absence makes the heart grow fonder" or "Out of sight, out of mind"?

Well, once Mom and Dad offered to pay for my plane ticket, all the worries quickly subsided, and I accepted the invitation to fly back and forth with Gramma. "Uncle Hank will bring you to the airport in Chicago, and we'll pick you up in West Palm Beach," my mother assured me over the phone. She was sitting in the air conditioning to beat the heat. I was sipping hot tea trying to get my feet warm.

"Yeah, Mom, I got it," I said as the steam from my tea cup fogged up my glasses. I imagined watching the hot air rise in a gentle haze from a white sand beach.

"Unfortunately, you'll have to transfer in Philadelphia." Mom sounded genuinely sorry. "At least there'll be enough time to help Gramma change planes." That meant a longish layover. I figured I could handle it. Unlike most of her grandchildren, I had grown up in Michigan three hours away from my grandmother. My visits with her had been precious but few, usually two or three times during the warmer months and once around the holidays. I could certainly make use of a little extra time with my grandmother.

Gramma Triezenberg was a truly old-fashioned grandmother. The new-fangled grandmothers including my children's grandmothers are like grey-haired versions of supermoms. They always have special kiddie goodies in the house. They have bought special toys to keep at their homes just for when the grandchildren come over to play. They can read story after story after story without seeming to mind. And if that isn't enough to endear them to my children, the new-fashioned grandmothers do things parents seldom do—take little kids to Dunkin Donuts, buy them carousel rides at the mall, and bring them to

McDonald's and let them eat only french fries for lunch. My Gramma didn't do any of those things. Disposable income was for her a contradiction in terms. But that didn't matter. Every time I showed up, there was a great big gramma-hug waiting for me. She loved me just because I was her grandchild and, of course, I loved her just because she was my gramma.

Once when I was a little girl, I got to stay at Gramma Triezenberg's for a few days while Mom and Dad were away somewhere. I don't remember much about my time there except that Gramma found some scrap material and sewed me a play skirt that hung all the way to the floor. For a few minutes she looked at me and then at her material. After that she spent an hour or two snipping and stitching, and, voilá, a little skirt that whirled just perfectly when I wore it and twirled around the living room. My mother remembers a younger Gramma Triezenberg staying up late into the nights, sewing clothes for her six children–Mom and her brothers and sisters. Gramma could even find a used coat that was two sizes too big for anyone, take apart each seam and remake the coat to fit someone in her family. No one ever guessed that those coats were remakes. Gramma's sewing was quality through and through. I wore that play skirt until the hemline was at my knees and I still have it folded neatly in a box in the closet. When my daughter Anika is a little older, I'll let her play with it, too. Gramma would want that. She was a no-nonsense woman, and there's no sense in keeping a perfectly good play skirt stuffed away in a box, when a darling little girl could be playing in it. Fifteen years after she sewed my skirt, Gramma's fingers and mind were still nimble enough to sew the dress she wore to my wedding. According to Gramma, those store-bought dresses never fit quite right. But by piecing several of her well-used patterns together, Gramma could whip up a dress that lay the way a dress ought to and had buttons that wouldn't come off even after several washings. Gramma looked great at our wedding in the solid blue dress she had made herself. That one was the last dress she ever sewed.

"Don't worry, Mom," I said into the phone a week later. It was my turn do some reassuring. "I already called ahead for a wheel chair at the Philadelphia airport." My mother, duly impressed that her daughter was learning something useful in graduate school, promised again to meet me at the airport in West Palm before hanging up.

In the year before my trip with Gramma, it became clear to everyone that Gramma's mind was slipping. So while en route Gramma was in charge of her purse, I was in charge of everything else. Fortunately, the pre-boarding call for those needing extra assistance was meant for Gramma and me. Once we were seated, Gramma sat quite properly holding her purse as the other passengers boarded. Shortly after take-off, Gramm leaned over and shook her head, "I dunno, Penny. This is the quietest bus I've ever been on."

"Gramma, this isn't a bus. You're in an airplane."

"An airplane?" She was visibly impressed with herself. "My father would never believe this." She was shaking her head again. When the drinks were served, Gramma chose coffee. I watched her carefully stir in her sugar and powdered creamer. Coffee drinking was an institution in the Triezenberg family. Every Sunday after morning church, someone hosted "coffee." When she was younger, Gramma would take her turn hosting. Her specialty was Boston brown bread. She would set out thick slices of the dark, rich bread and make coffee on the gas stove in the all-glass percolator. Whenever we visited, I would eat my brown bread, raisins and all, and watch with fascination as Grampa stirred half-n-half into his cup and then poured the coffee back and forth between his coffee cup and an ice cream saucer. Gramma was the opposite of snooty, but she was neat and dainty in her own way and opted to stir her coffee until it was cool enough to drink. Even at ninety, Gramma sat primly stirring her coffee with the plastic straw.

**

In all my courses in grad school, no one had ever told me to pack lots of dollar bills along to tip people when you travel. When we landed in Philadelphia, I had to get rid of the young man who protected the wheelchair.

"Gramma, why don't we go to the bathroom now. Then we won't have to go in the plane." She thought that was a good idea, and I quickly took charge of the chair and pushed her towards the women's restroom. The now chairless man disappeared in search of someone who wasn't in graduate school and knew to be prepared to tip all the helpers of the airport world.

I helped Gramma out of the wheel chair and into a bathroom stall. "I'll wait right outside your door, Gramma. If you need any help, just yell." I waited patiently. It was very quiet in there, and I wondered what all a grandmother needs to do in an airport bathroom.

Finally, I heard a flush and Gramma poked her head out of the door. "Penny," she whispered. "Do you need to go to the bathroom, too?"

"Yeah, I'll wait until you're done," I answered.

Gramma peered around like she had a secret. Then she motioned for me to come into the stall. When I peeked in, I saw the toilette seat meticulously and neatly wrapped in toilet paper. One long strip lay on each side, and smaller pieces of paper were fitted and tucked in around the back and over the front tips. I've never seen anything quite like it since. "Look," whispered Gramma. "It's all still clean and dry, so you can use it. Then you won't have to mess with all that yourself." She patted my shoulder as she stepped past me and went to wash her hands.

I closed the stall door and looked at Gramma's handiwork. I thought about just flushing away the whole lot of little paper squares, but then I decided that Gramma was right. Reusing is a good thing, even if it is toilet paper. So I proceeded to appreciate Gramma's work of art in an appropriate way.

On the next leg of our trip, Gramma was once again impressed by how quiet the modern-day buses were. "No, Gramma, you're in a plane. You're flying to Florida to visit Ben and Ruthie."

"I'm going to Florida?" Gramma was surprised. "Imagine that. Me in Florida!" I don't know if Gramma had ever been farther away from her home than the family vacations to Minnesota. But I'm quite sure that Florida qualified as very far away indeed.

"Yup," I nodded. "Aunt Dorothy and Uncle Mel are there, too." I don't think it ever really occurred to my grandmother to be skeptical or mistrusting or pessimistic, but I wanted to assure her that her granddaughter was taking her somewhere meaningful.

"Well, that's nice," she said as she settled into her seat. "You know," she said closing her eyes. "This is the quietest bus ride I've ever been on."

***

When we arrived in West Palm Beach, my aunt and uncle and my parents met us at the airport. "Welcome to Florida, Ma!" said my Uncle Mel as he grabbed the carry-on.

Gramma's face lit up. "It's good to see you, Mel. And Dorothy." Everyone exchanged kisses and hugs. "Ruthie, there you are! Hi, Ben." Gramma wore a big smile.

My dad Ben asked, "How was the trip, Ma?"

"Quiet," said Gramma shaking her head.

On the car ride to my parents' mobile home, Gramma peered out her window. "Everything's so green, ain't it?"

"Well, Mother," said my mom. "It's warm here. You're in Florida now."

"I'm in Florida?" Gramma was surprised. "Imagine that!" Several times that week, we needed to remind Gramma of where she was and of how she got there. "Boy," she commented once after figuring out again that she actually was in Florida. "It's rough being past the line."

I looked at her. "You mean 'over the hill'?" I asked.

"Yeah. Over the hill. Boy, you get dumber fast. Faster and faster. Going up is slow, man, slow. But once you're going down, well, watch out!" Gramm was smiling and shaking her head. "At least you're smarter going down."

"But, Gramma," I interrupted. "You just said you got dumber."

"Well," she looked thoughtful. "You got all those experiences–a whole bag full. The problem is you can't keep them straight." She tapped her head with her pointer finger. "They're all crooked in there."

Gramma knew she was losing it, and in her gentle way, she let us know that she knew. Once after breakfast, I had just reminded her again that she was staying at Ben and Ruthie's in Florida. She looked at me with big eyes. "You mean, I slept here last night? Boy, I don't remember a thing." She was shaking her head and smiling good-naturedly. "Well, I'm real appreciative." She paused and then added with a twinkle in her eye, "That I don't remember!"

I laughed. "You appreciate that you don't remember?"

Gramma laughed, too. "You gotta make a joke of it, Penny, because that's what it is." I lost count of how many times we told Gramma that she was in Florida. She didn't seem to care really where she was, but the whole week her face wore a smile because she was spending time with her family.

***

For the first half of the Florida getaway, Gramma slept at my parents' place. She got the guestroom, and I slept on the sofa. This arrangement was fine by me. I could stay up late, phone my hubby, and mill about the kitchen and living room until I felt like going to bed. Once Gramma and my parents retired to their bedrooms, I had the run of the place, or so I thought. The first night I had just gotten to sleep when a beam of light shone right in my eyes. I sat up and tried to block the brightness with my arm. Then I heard a small voice whispering, "Is that you, Penny?" It was Gramma investigating her surroundings by flashlight.

"Yeah, Gramma, it's me. Are you okay?"

"Yeah. Boy, am I glad it's you. Where am I?" She had walked over to the sofa and was shining the light into my face.

"You're at Ben and Ruthie's, Gramma, in Florida. Remember?"

"Oh yeah." She nodded slowly.

"Come on," I said getting up. "I'll help you back to your bedroom." After I tucked her in, I set the flashlight next to her bed. "Good-night, Gramma." I said giving her a kiss on the cheek.

"Thanks, Penny. Good-night, now." she said. The same thing happened the next two nights. At some point in the middle of the night, Gramma would meander into the living room and find me asleep on the sofa. Then I would remind her of where she was and help her back into bed. The third night she sat on the edge of her bed shaking her head. "Sorry, I woke you up, Penny," she said.

"That's okay, Gramma. Let's get you back into bed," I said taking the familiar flashlight out of her hands.

"You know," she said lifting her legs gingerly onto the bed. "You get a little crazier every day."

I yawned and chuckled. "I'm glad you said it and not me!" I smiled.

Gramma looked at me as I fluffed her pillow. "Watch out!" she said pointing a finger at me. "You're on the way!" We both laughed quietly so we wouldn't wake up anyone else. Of course, she was right. We're all bound to get a little crazier every day. If we manage to do so with the gentle spirit of Gramma Triezenberg, then that crazy world won't be so bad.

I said good-night and shut her door behind me. As I made my way back to the sofa, it occurred to me that twenty years ago it was Gramma tucking me in for the night, but even back then, I was stuck sleeping on the sofa.

* * *

I used to stop by Gramma's house on my trips from Madison, Wisconsin, to Michigan. She would serve me a can of Campbell's vegetable soup, or I would take her out to Russ', a family restaurant which serves up basic food at good prices *and* closed on Sundays. (For those reasons that restaurant was frequented by all the West Michigan and South Holland Dutch Americans lucky enough to be within driving distance of a franchise.) I remember once over pie and coffee, I asked Gramma about her and Grampa and how they met. Evidently Grampa came riding over in a car one day and was honking the horn in the driveway, just like a teenager. Gramma was trying to sound annoyed at Grampa's behavior, but she was smiling when she told me. "He was dressed real nice. And the other boy with him too." She paused. "I told my sister I did not want to go driving with that John Triezenberg. But Johanna said I really ought to. That it'd be fun. Well," Gramma said and shrugged. "That's how it began."

Another time I remember her telling me that when she married Grampa, she knew he was the only one for her. "I told him, I did: 'John, I'm never marrying anyone else.' And he said to me, 'What are you talking about, woman? What if something happens to me? You might want to remarry!' And I shook my head and said, 'No, John, I'm never marrying anyone else.' And I didn't." Grampa had died of a heart attack several years back. I was trying to remember exactly when that was, when Gramma stood up and waved her hand. "Aw, heah," she said. "After being married, who wants to get to know another man and have him watch you get undressed and all that. Heah, who needs it!"

When Gramma was staying at my parents' in Florida, body bronzing on the beaches and walking tours of the local sights were not on the agenda. I can't remember exactly what we did all day. But I know I listened a lot to Gramma. It was different than stopping by her place for a one-hour visit because you had the leisure to just be together and let your thinking turn into words slowly. While we twiddled those few days away together, I learned, for example, that Gramma knew more songs by heart than I do. One morning she was telling me how much she enjoyed songs in church. Then she began singing:

"The more you find Him precious true,
the more you know what He can do for you.
What will you do without Him,
when He has shut the door?"

There were many other songs with lines like, "Jesus is more, is more to me" and "I'll go where you want me to go, dear Lord," and

"How can you not want a Savior?
How can you not want a friend?
Jesus will love you faithfully
until the end."

Gramma would sing her ditties morning, noon and night. "You know, Penny," she said to me between songs one morning. "My mind keeps traveling. It don't stand still!"

Most of her songs were church songs. But sometimes she would rattle off little songs or poems that she had learned as a small girl. One of her school ditties went like this:

Round and round it goes.
Dripping, dropping, rolling wheel
that turns the noisy rusty well.
Round and round it goes.
Round and round it goes.

I have no idea where these poems came from, and she probably didn't either. But they had made their way into her memory, and they were not leaving any time soon. Some were impressively long, like the "little leaves" one.

"I'll tell you how the leaves came down,"
the great tree to its children said.
"You're getting sleepy yellow and brown.
Yes, very sleepy little red.
It's quite time you went to bed."

"Ah," begged each silly pouting leaf.
"Let us a little longer stay.
Dear Father tree, behold our grief.
It's such a very pleasant day.
We do not want to go away."

So for just one more merry day
the great tree to its leaflets clung.
They frolicked and danced and had their way
upon the autumn breezes swung
whispering all their sports among.

Amazingly Gramma could remember every line of that children's poem, and I had to ask her several times to repeat things so that I could write it down. Nevertheless, the next minute I had to remind her that she was in Florida visiting Ruthie.

During those couple days, Gramma shared more than songs and ditties. She seemed to want to leave me with some gramma wisdom. She told me how before she married Grampa, she had wanted to go to work in the corset factory in Chicago. The pastor who had stopped by to discuss things with her father asked, "Do you trust her in Chicago?"

Her father wisely replied, "Hattie?" (Gramma's name was Henrietta, but everyone called her Hattie for short.) "I'd trust her anywhere." Gramma was very proud that her father trusted her and that he outright told that pastor so.

"That my dad trusted me...that affected me a lot." Gramma was rocking gently in the recliner. "I was a good kid. I heard enough without seeing any of it. I suppose young people must fail sometimes because it's not easy. But my dad trusted me. That meant a lot." She kept rocking slowly. "Never steal, Penny. I never stole. I was never in a movie house either. Grandpa worked hard and talked about a dime show like in the funny papers. Maybe movies are better or more sophisticated, but maybe they're just worse. Anyway, they're not so good from what I hear." She closed her eyes and I thought she was drifting to sleep when her eyes opened. "You know, Penny, some kids don't want to listen until they get in the soup kettle." She closed her eyes again and then added, "Sometimes you do something wrong. And sometimes you pay for it the rest of your life." I wondered if Gramma was thinking of anything in particular, but she had begun to breathe deeply, so I tiptoed from the living room and left her in peace.

Later that day over afternoon coffee, she was talking more about her family. "Ya know," she said. "Family can get under your skin. You can say, 'I don't like this one or that one or them two.' I dunno. Maybe they like one more than the other, but they know they belong together. That's family."

Gramma had raised a family that stuck together. Not only did her six children keep in touch and see each other regularly, for years the same group who met every Sunday after morning worship for coffee would take their vacations together. Everyone would pack their families and half their kitchens and drive to northern Minnesota. For one or two weeks most of the Triezenberg clan would park themselves at some lucky cabin resort on Long Lake. There were fishing contests and pig roasts, shopping sprees which always ended with pie and coffee in the local café, water skiing and paddle boat rides. During vacation, "coffee" didn't happen after Sunday morning worship. "Coffee" was every night after it got too dark to fish. Each evening one family would host "coffee" in their cabin and then several games would start up in different cabins and go until late into the night. Some of the aunts and uncles would be playing May-I or pinochle while the cousins enjoyed hearts or Uno. Gramma would just sit and sip her coffee and chat with whoever happened to sit by her. She didn't play the games. She just enjoyed being with the people. So, it didn't matter really that we didn't do much during those sunny days in Florida. Gramma could just enjoy being with family.

At the midway point in our spring break, Gramma was scheduled to move from my parents' mobile home to Aunt Dorothy's, which was one street over in the same mobile home park. (Proof positive that the family togetherness extended easily into the retirement years.) At bedtime in her last evening by us, Gramma had finished in the bathroom and invited me to have my turn. I went in and began brushing my teeth when I noticed that the bathroom door leading to the guest room was ajar. Gramma was sitting on the edge of her bed mumbling. I finished brushing and went to shut the door, when I realized that Gramma was praying. "Guide me in Thy ways. Bless and keep all my children and grandchildren." As I quietly turned the knob, I smiled. Gramma was praying for me, too. While I shut the door, I listened to her pray. "Keep me from sin, Lord. And, bless Johanna. Is she still alive? I don't even know." I tried not to laugh, as Gramma continued. "Well, *you* know. If she's alive, Lord, then bless Johanna." I wanted to go about my bathroom business, but I was riveted by Gramma's simple praying. "Bless and keep all my children and grandchildren." I realized she was beginning to repeat herself. In a way, it was nice to know she was talking with God just like she talked with everyone else. "May they all come to a saving knowledge of you." I wondered how often she had prayed those words. "And forgive my sins, Lord. I don't try to do wrong, but I pray your forgiveness for the wrong I do." I could not imagine trustworthy little Hattie or

Henrietta the young seamstress-mother, or my own white-haired Gramma, ever doing anything rough or mean or wrong. "Not for my sake but for Jesus' sake, Amen."

As quietly as I could, I released the doorknob and let it click into place. When I returned to my bathroom duties, I noticed that the toilet seat wasn't dressed delicately in fresh toilet paper. It didn't matter. Gramma's love still filled the room because her prayers for her six children and twenty-some grandchildren including me lingered there.

During her last night by us, she didn't get out of bed to pay me a visit. On Wednesday Gramma moved from my parents' mobile home to Aunt Dorothy's. I sent the flashlight along with her just in case she needed it. But according to my Aunt Dorothy, Gramma never once got out of bed at night during her half week stay at their place.

* * *

Once Gramma left, I got to sleep in the guestroom. Mom and Dad took me sightseeing, and I even got to spend part of a day on the beach. But things weren't the same without Gramma. Fortunately, we ate almost all our dinners together with her and Aunt Dorothy and Uncle Mel. On the ride home from the restaurant one night I got to hear about how fast Gramma was when she was a little girl. She could run and run and run and not be tired at all. On another night, she reminisced about her days helping in the ice cream parlor. In one of the restaurants, she leaned over to me and said, "You know, you can't always say what you want, even if you want to." I had no idea what she was talking about, but I remembered what she said.

On the flight home, I had Gramma to myself again. This time she didn't talk about how quiet the bus ride was. She was surprised though several times to realize she was actually up in the air. Gramma had a middle seat. I sat on the aisle to Gramma's left and a pleasant, dark-haired woman had the window seat on Gramma's right. When the flight attendant brought us our plastic trays of culinary delights, Gramma bowed her head to pray. I followed suit and after a minute or so I found myself waiting patiently for Gramma to finish. She was taking quite a while, and the woman in the window seat eventually leaned forward and whispered to me, "Is she okay?"

Quick as a flash, Gramma opened one eye and looked at me. Then she closed her eyes again. I nodded assuringly to our concerned row-mate and shrugged my shoulders. Another minute later Gramma opened her eyes and licked her lips. "I was just praying," she declared to both of us. Then she leaned towards the friendly stranger and said with a wink, "I prayed for you, too."

The young woman sat up with a surprised look on her face, but that expression quickly mellowed to a warm smile. "Well, thank you," she said as we all began eating our supper.

That was Gramma–simple gentility, unfailing love, no-nonsense practicality, unwavering faith. It took a spring break in Florida with her to make me realize what a successful life this unassuming woman had led. I want to grow old like she did, to see my children and grandchildren and great grandchildren grow into themselves and into healthy traditions centered on family and grounded in faith.

About ten weeks after Gramma and I returned from Florida, she left us all and got to go to her real home. I like to imagine her up there singing all the praise songs in the book from perfect memory, sipping coffee with Grampa and Great Aunt Johanna, and waiting patiently for the rest of us to join her. After all, family belongs together.

**

Henrietta Tanis Triezenberg
1903-1993

Carroll D. Yoder

THE MIDDLE ROLL

At six o'clock on the seventh of June, six people were eating supper—egg dutch, apple sauce, fried potatoes, Grandma's fresh bread. Six cinnamon rolls with burnt sugar frosting filled a pan on the table. Strange that almost everything was turning into sixes—even the rolls. Usually a pan had seven. Darrell counted them again—five fat women, their rear ends hanging over the edge and one huge middle roll inside. The middle roll—the one everybody wanted.

If Papa took the first one, Russell the second, and Norman the third, there would be no problem. With half the pan gone, Darrell would have the right to the big roll in the center. Already he could feel the frosting, brown and sweet, on his fingers—extra frosting that slid into the middle one from the rolls around it.

"For once the frosting turned out right," Mama said. She was always fussing about the frosting. It either got too hard and sugary and fell off in little pieces when you dunked it in the hot chocolate or it was too sticky.

If Mama started the rolls around the table, Norman was sure to grab the middle one. The pan was sitting close to Papa's place—a good sign except that Papa had more food left on his plate than anyone else and might not take the first roll. If Davy helped himself first, Russell would be the lucky person.

"Those rolls look extra good—really big," Russell said. He was looking at Davy. It wasn't fair because Darrell had helped Mama with the rolls in the afternoon. Mama always made cinnamon rolls every Saturday, seven pans, and they tasted the best of all on Saturday night. Mama hadn't even asked for his help.

"I don't know how a person is supposed to get everything done on Saturday with a Sunday School lesson to teach and company coming tomorrow for dinner and Davy and Norman's baths to give yet and my good mixer on the blink. Won't even have so much as time to lie down for ten minutes." Mama was working lickety-split, spreading butter and sprinkling sugar and cinnamon on the rolled-out dough.

That was when Darrell said, "I could cut the rolls and put them in the pans for you." And Mama looked up, surprised and grateful at the same time. So he took the thread that she kept in the second drawer and slipped it under the long roll of dough and pulled both ends away from each other so that the each roll came apart without squashing. Because he cut the first ones a little too wide, tonight's pan had only six. He knew that he deserved the middle roll. No one else had helped Mama—helped without even being asked.

Davy reached for the first roll. "Wait a minute!" Mama ordered. "I haven't even poured the hot chocolate and Papa's plate is half full yet." Russell looked disappointed. Maybe Mama knew that Darrell was counting on the middle roll.

"I think Papa should get the first roll," Darrell said. "He works harder than anybody else, unless Mama."

"But it's hard for little boys to wait." Papa smiled at Davy. He knew that three-year-olds liked to dig out the first roll by themselves.

"Well, he can wait until I get the hot chocolate." Mama got up to go to the stove. Papa was still eating. "Give me your cup," Mama said to Davy. "Be careful, it's hot!"

And then without asking he tore out the first roll, his fingers dripping with frosting, his eager hand almost spilling the hot chocolate. The second went to Mama, the third to Papa.

"I get the middle one!" Russell's face glowed.

"Not so fast!" Darrell's hand grabbed across the table as Russell pulled the pan back, knocking over a cup of hot chocolate.

"Now, look what you've done! A person can't even eat supper in peace after working hard all day. And I'm the one that has to clean it up." Mama was on her feet, looking for the dish rag.

"Not my fault," Russell said. "It was my roll and Darrell tried to take it away from me."

"You always manage somehow to get the middle one, but not tonight because I did the work this afternoon. I cut all the rolls and put them in the pans." Darrell could defend himself.

"Yes, and I appreciated that," Mama said coming back to the table. "By rights, you should have had it. But you didn't help me just so that you could have the middle roll, did you?"

"Oh, take it, then." Darrell glared at his brother. "I don't want it anyway."

Anne Hoffman

EZEKIEL

We went to the slopes along that river every day
waiting for signs - for floods, or storms
or hope in any form. Even so, we were surprised by its
appearance.

Just as the air grew damp and hot
Just as breaths burned and stopped half-formed
Just as they all turned south toward the city

                              Just as I looked north.
Just like any dark cloud it pushed its head
above the distant hills.

There was no sound until the wind whined high
and hard. Clothing flapped around me.
All those robes and wraps sounded like clapping.
No one spoke when the wind stopped. Silence
framed the whole event. But I was not alone.
No matter what they tell you,

                              I was not alone.
We all stood there looking up, while creatures
made from clouds and flesh danced above us.

Don't you sing that I alone saw some wheel
way up high in the middle of the sky

                              because they were there
watching with me.

However,
only I thought it real, only I turned sleepless
after sleepless night into a lifestyle ranting.
Only I whirled those words like wheels inside my chest
and hurt forever from the pressure which even the
aftertaste of honey lingering on my gums could not
                    erase.

Deborah Bowen

IN THE BEGINNING
A parable of Southern England

In the beginning it was easy enough for them to talk of gardens. To consider the relative merits of hollyhocks and delphiniums; to recommend nasturtiums or rosemary for sunny borders; to weigh candytuft against bachelor's buttons, pinks against aubretia; to pinch snapdragons and bruise lavender between finger and thumb. In the beginning the narrow stream shimmered under the old stone bridge, and below the surface of the pond huge goldfish gaped and glowed beneath the flat capacious foliage of water-lilies.

Even to come to such a place was a gift, a miracle, to Sharon, whose daily life was now gardenless and surrounded by nondescript city concrete. And to Adam any beginning in flowers was fine. He blossomed between the herbaceous borders where he could forget the mess of his relationship with his father and the tensions with Evelyn that had arisen even before they left the country to settle for a house in town. Childhood and adolescence for both Sharon and Adam, they discovered, had been filled with country garden flowers. They smiled, peering into the distance through the cascading rose-arches. Sharon felt moved to begin keeping a journal. Adam decided to extend his weekend arts retreat into the following week.

But time is relentless and unbound. Even hollyhocks grow tired, and roses shed petals in the rain. Before long the pinks browned and the delphiniums drooped. While Adam flirted in the lavender, pretending to paint, Evelyn, having organized a sitter who could handle three small children overnight, took off to Paris through the chunnel on a British Rail Special.

"Daddy," pleaded Seth over the phone a week later, "Mummy isn't here and I don't like fish. Please tell Mrs Jimson that I don't have to eat it."

"Mrs Jimson? What's she doing there?" Adam was put out. He had barely given Evelyn or the children a second thought since his arrival in Wiltshire. He had phoned home only on the first evening, out of some vestigial sense of duty. "Where is Mummy? Is she okay?"

"She said she was going on a train," said Seth. "I don't remember where." Not even beginning to suspect the effect of his words. "Daddy, you know what? Cam wet his bed again! Mrs Jimson got cross. And can I have pizza for breakfast? She says Heaven knows, I have to ask you."

Adam made the requisite fatherly noises and put down the phone rather thoughtfully. He went to find Sharon in the herb-garden. She was doing a pastel drawing in bright fuzzy colours. Adam discovered that he was annoyed.

"I really don't think you can claim to see any shocking pinks around here — or is this a cubist deconstruction?" he snapped.

Sharon looked up, surprised.

"Look, I have to go back to London. Family stuff. I wondered if you'd come with me. I'd like you to meet my children. And my wife, of course."

Sharon considered.

"Actually I'm paid up for another two days here. But the gardens are rather past their best now, aren't they? And I don't have to be back at work till Tuesday." The pastel crayon held lightly to her mouth like a child's sugar cigarette. Adam's exquisite garden a magnet. "Oh, well, thank you, then. You think your wife wouldn't mind an unexpected guest? Your part of London certainly sounds like an improvement on mine — I'm only in Kilburn because of the office."

She smiled gratefully. Adam recognized a victory, here at least.

"Good, that's settled then. Could you be ready by three? There's a fast train into Paddington at half past."

He walked quickly back to the house, brushing against the faded holly-hocks at the gate, crushing rosepetals underfoot.

***

The journey home was uneventful. They caught the train and sped towards the city. Sharon had poked lavender into her button-hole; Adam had acquired a rooted sprig of early Tudor rosemary for his rock-garden. They took the grubby commuter train out to Blackheath. At the house Seth greeted them joyfully and incuriously, and led Sharon into the extraordinarily messy living-room to show her the goldfish. "But they eat each other sometimes," he added with wide-eyed horror.

Cam was dropping bits of white paper into the aquarium. Abby asked, "Are you our Daddy's new friend?"

Sharon felt foolish. The absence of Evelyn was tangibly present, and Adam was offering no explanation at all.

"Well, I suppose," she said to Abby. And, after a pause, "Shall we make some dinner?" Food seemed a safe and possibly redemptive next step. She intuited, correctly, that Adam was unlikely to invade the kitchen.

Evelyn had sent a card of the Seine to the children. "Paris is very hot! I like the river, but it's a bit smelly. Love you all lots — Mum xoxoxo." How much use was that, thought Adam. Not, of course, that it was aiming to be useful.

Mrs Jimson pointed out that she had been paid only for the one night, and had now spent six. "But I couldn't just leave them without a soul, now, could I? And their gran with that bad leg, even if she *could* see her way to come over." Giving a sniff.

Adam handed over a sizeable cheque and closed the door on her. He sat down. In his head he could hear his father's voice, counselling a recognition of blame. Evelyn deserving his attention more often. Parenting as a two-person job. Etcetera. He tuned the voice out and went up to his study.

Horticultural magazines spilled all over his desk. He thought about propagating from the rosemary sprig. How much, how fast, which buyers. He thought about Sharon in the kitchen with Abby. How easy it seemed.

***

Although, of course, this was only the first evening. He remembered suddenly and unwillingly the white rosebush that he had planted in his father's garden for Evelyn on their first ecstatic visit. And what was she up to now, in Paris? Things had been easy with Evelyn too, in the beginning.

Alan Berecka

STONE COMFORT

It has been one year.
The earth has sunk; the grass
has finally taken. The dreams—
memories of the pain—her pain—
her
   (in the last months
when the cancer found her
spine, even the pumped morphine
could not ease her, nor end
her labor which unlike
the grayed Sara came to no end
but her prolonged own)
               seem less real
than this stone, a cold and chiseled
reality, which I come here to speak
with and take comfort from. That I find
this strange does not seem to matter.

My daughter, now three,
has never seen this stone. She
has been taught a wooden truth
that she has two grandmothers, one down
South, one up in heaven. To me
this seems too soft, a truth
that bears too little suffering.
Perhaps, someday, she too will find
comfort in stone.

Chet Corey

MEN AT CHURCH

The men are angry at the women
playing at church the way girls
have always played at dress up.
For the men, the liturgy is more
like watching girls run or throw
a baseball—girls who never could
grasp the intricacies of football,
girls who shivered at sidelines,
waved their pompoms and signaled
to their heroes in a private code
of promise if they should score.
On Sunday mornings, the piano
bench is reserved for the spreading
warmth of a woman, say the men;
places in the choir, for their voices;
not the altar side for first or second
reading; and never the homily—"By God,"
the angry men say, "never the homily."

Leslie Winfield Williams

DEATH DANCE OF THE RED SHOES

"And if your right hand causes you to sin, cut it offand throw it away; it is better that you lose one of your members than your whole body go into hell."

Matthew 5:30

and
the red shoes danced
Karen
on
and on

scarlet slippers
of untoward
desire,
shuffle-bar-hopping,
flinging,
pirouetting her
over forest floors
of lichen and spackled light—
kicking up glossy
pine needle rug
patches

those red pumps
ferocious,
never skipping a beat,
through days
and nights
and evenings of purple
crepuscular
sighs,
whirling Karen in
a tarantella
down dusty roads
across fields flowered, thistled
with prickly leaves
to sting, to whip

her legs, hairless
and innocent
and

on
and on
the shoes danced
Karen
deep into a night
so blotted
she saw only blobs of sin
at the end
of her feet

so the hangman
chopped them off
for her,
built sturdy members
instead,
but the foot-stubs
still oozed
charm, red
in the moonlight
glinting
off the patent leather
toes

with new,
less troublesome feet,
Karen finally
died,
and the rose angel
who came to get her
never asked
about shoes, red
or otherwise

Gail White

PALM SUNDAY

No doubt we meant to be great things –
industry captains, corporate kings,
scientists, artists, authors – such
ambitions show we thought too much.

Stunning success was hard to find.
We flopped, and said we didn't mind.
The roof above our visions leaked –
was it in college that we peaked?

One day we almost heard the cheers
that sang Hosanna in our ears,
turned round, and we were half-way through
the same dark forest Dante knew.
Those trees were cut to build our cross.
Dear loser, help us bear our loss.

Gail White

YOUNG SKEPTIC

My great-aunt asked me what I'd like for Easter
(I was seven) and I said, "A dress of lace."
It wasn't lace. It was buttercup-yellow cotton
with an organdy pinafore, lace-trimmed on the edges.
I'll say for me, I hid my disappointment.
Even at seven I knew I should be grateful
to my aunt, who made scraped beef when I was sick
and did her best to save my black kitten's life
when it was obviously not meant to live,
who always let me play dress-up with her clothes
and let me raid her bookshelves on demand.
We could talk pets or parents or religion.

But it wasn't lace. And in my Easter gloom
I first had doubts about the empty tomb.

Myrna Downer

BEAUTIFUL WHISPER

In the end it's the
beautiful whisper
the shy child
whose voice is seldom heard
but you recognize it
none the less
in arctic blossoms,
a new baby clinging to your finger
the first song you learned to strum
and the passionate way
your God moves closer

These are dark times
but even darkness
has its rightful season
Sound moves deeper there
Ask any who've been truly lost
Who was it that conquered the
second death?

Only the honest will admit
to the
beautiful whisper
in the night

Sharon Dunn

IN THE HALF CIRCLE, WHEN YOU ARE GONE

This is real. The sky glows with a pink sunrise. Out my window, I can see Mr. Jenson's tulips in his flower box, patches of pink and yellow. I wonder what he does with his time. He never weeds his plants.

The glider rocker creaks harmoniously with Monique's gentle sucking at my breast. She stares at me with wide, unblinking eyes and wraps her finger around my pinky. The soft spot on her head moves up and down with the rhythm of her nursing. She studies me—big round eyes. Her irises are the deepest brown I've ever seen.

We are allies in the battle for her to adjust to life outside of me. She slept in two hour blocks, waking to nurse and be held. We have made it through another night.

I whisper as she watches me, "Yes, I'm your Mama. Get to know this face. It's the face that will always take care of you. Yes, baby."

She detaches and coos at me, her mouth in a perfect 'O' shape, a teaspoon of milk visible inside the pocket of her cheek.

This is not real. I am at the mall. Derek is watching Monique, so I can buy some new clothes. As I ride the escalator down, my mother's laughter passes me going up.

I turn, pushing people aside to get up the down escalator. Like a fading perfume, I hear the laughter again and follow. Ahead is a woman with brown hair drawn back into a bun, my mother. My heart beating and sweat running down my back, I lose sight of her in the crowd. I eliminate the people one head at a time; she has to be there. The surge of tightness through my own breasts reminds me that I need to get home and nurse Monique. I survey the throng of people one more time. I can't find her, and the loss makes me feel like an abandoned house with the wind blowing through it—hollow woman. I walk past the shops, unable to remember why I came here. I need to get home to Monique, that's all I know.

I'm pretty sure this is not real. Derek grips my hand so tight that it hurts. He nods as the psychiatrist talks to us.

"I think this has gone beyond postpartum, Mrs. Mallery. Your mother's death and the birth of your daughter coming so close together have caused a severe depression...and some other problems." His voice fades.

Saying the death and birth were close together is an understatement. While my mother lay dying in a cancer hospital two hundred miles away, I was giving birth to Monique. I wasn't there to comfort my mother. I never saw her dead. I never said good-bye.

I can hear my daughter crying in the next room. The secretary has agreed to hold her so we could have this "conference." Conference, ha! It's more like an ambush. Monique's cry rises up through the closed door. I want to go to her.

"So Mrs. Mallery, Derek is going to help you remember to take your Zoloft everyday."

My awareness snaps away from my child and back into the room. "I told you before, I'm not taking any of that stuff while I'm nursing Monique."

"You can wean the kid. She is six months old," Derek says.

"She's not 'the kid', Derek, she's Monique, your daughter." He wanted a boy. That's why he hasn't bonded with Monique. I look directly at the psychiatrist. "I'm not taking the happy pills."

"Your husband has expressed some concern about your safety…and your baby's."

"She leaves the stove on, forgets to lock the doors. Things, valuable things, have been disappearing in the house. She doesn't know what happened to them."

My chest tightens. This must be what a deer feels like when the red dot of a hunter's laser scope fixes on the muscles and hide on top of her heart. "I'm not taking the pills. I don't care how jumbled my thinking is. It'll come back to me, where I put the video camera and your mother's stupid ring. I told you. I've been organizing, making room for Monique's stuff."

Dr. Siteris runs a hand through his stringy, red hair. Freckles populate his bald spot, and his skin has the paleness of a man who spends too much time under fluorescent lights. "All right, I can't make you take the medication. Do one thing for me. Write your mother a good-bye letter."

This is real and not real. I sit cross-legged on the porch and write the letter to my mother while Monique lies on a blanket. The sun warms my cheeks and arms. Monique holds her head up and reaches for the toys I've set out for her. The softest of breezes touches her downy dark head.

I found a piece of computer scratch paper to write on. I don't need to use good stationary for this stupid exercise.

I start to write. It's quiet this time of day in the neighborhood. Only Mr. Jenson next door and Mrs. Erinburg across the street are ever home. Mr. Jensen works at home making rough pine furniture he sells on the Internet and Mrs. Erinburg is a retired widow. When Monique was born, Mrs. Erinburg brought her a beautiful handmade quilt and Mr. Jenson brought her a wooden chair. I don't know how he makes any money with his furniture because the chair he gave us wobbles.

The letter starts out okay. I tell my mother I miss her. I talk about some of the things we used to do together, how I miss horseback riding and sewing and reading the same books together. Then I tell her about Monique, how beautiful she is. The words on the page get larger, distorted. I push my pencil so hard into the paper it tears. My vision blurs, and I can't see what I've written. I can't finish the letter. I wad it up and throw it in the garbage outside.

Later that day, while Monique sleeps, I look for the stuff I've misplaced, especially my mother-in-law's ring. If I can just remember what I did with that,

Derek will get off my back. I can do this without medication. I'll just have to double check the stove and always go back to see if I've locked the house after I put Monique in her car seat, which I hate doing. I hate leaving her alone on the street for even a minute. I worry that someone will take her. I hate leaving her alone in her bed. I'm afraid she will stop breathing, and I won't be there to rush her to the hospital. Some nights I lie on the floor beside her crib, so if she stops breathing or chokes, I'll be right there. Derek says I am irrational.

This is real. This is so very real. My mother is not dead. The email flashes on the screen. It's from my mother.

I've had this feeling before. Sometimes I'll wake in the night and I have the sense that she is alive. All I have to do is drive to her and she will be there in her house ...waiting for me...waiting for me to show her Monique, whom she has never seen.

I touch my hand to the computer screen. She describes her favorite recipe, pineapple upside-down cake. She talks about going horseback riding, about my horse Pepper. This is my mother.

I get four more emails from her. I don't tell Derek about them. The final email tells me to come to a grassy meadow outside of town. We both know it well. Mama wants to go riding with me. I pull the riding gear out of a downstairs closet and haul it to the car. Monique is still sleeping, I can go back for her after I get the saddle in the trunk. Just as I close the trunk, Mrs. Erinburg's car revs to life. She waves at me as she passes by.

But when I go back to get Monique, the door is locked. Sweat from my palms makes the knob sticky as I grip it, shake it. I know I didn't lock the doors. Why would I lock my own daughter in? Because I do not know what else to do, I check my pocket for keys that are not there. Why would I lock the doors? I never remember to lock the door.

I run along the stone path to the back door. I cannot explain the need I have to know that my daughter is safe, always safe, to lean over her crib in the dark holding my breath so I can hear her breathing. I cannot explain the anxiety that rises up when someone else holds her even if they stay in the same room where I can see her. I feel it in the soreness of my breasts, but also in my shaking hand, hands that are not holding her right now.

The back door is locked too. I know I didn't lock it...or did I? She is in there alone. What if she wakes up and no one is there to hold her, to make her feel safe?

I whirl around. Mr. Jenson's shop door is ajar. Maybe I could use his phone to call a locksmith. I race across the yard. "Mr. Jensen are you in there? I have an minor emergency." I try to sound calm, taking deep breaths in between sentences.

The big wooden door screeches when I push it open. Inside, there is no light save for the glow from his computer. Pine boards are stacked against the wall beside a saw, but there is no sign of furniture being made, no half finished chair, no cut boards, no completed furniture. I pull on the chain for the bare bulb hanging from the ceiling, light floods the corners of the workshop. I see the video camera first, stored next to a Coleman lantern and down sleeping bag. I remember the college student across the street saying something about camping gear missing from his car. My feet pad across the concrete floor. A tight cord of anxiety twists my chest and stomach.

In the middle of the shelves is a shoe box. My hands trembling, I lift it off the shelf and open it. Inside, amongst other rings and necklaces, is my mother-in-law's ruby ring that she gave me as an heirloom for Monique.

I can't breath.

Still clutching the box, I make my way toward the door. As I pass the computer, I see the crumpled pieces of paper that have been smoothed out, the letter to my mother, the pharmacy's instructions for taking the Zoloft. I flip the letter over; my email address is on the back.

I can feel my pulse thudding in my neck as I look through another stack of papers, the stained recipe for pineapple upside-down cake where I've hand written "mother's favorite recipe." I threw it out after I transferred all the recipes to the computer. Also in the pile is a torn picture of me with my horse. Pepper's name is written on the back of the photograph. My pulse thuds in my ears. My breath is shallow, wheezy.

I drop the box of jewelry and run back to the house. I did this to my daughter. I traded the fantasy of my mother being alive for my baby's safety. He's in the house. He thought Mrs. Erinburg's car pulling away was me. Please, dear God, let Monique still be asleep, don't let him find her. He has to have been upstairs where she sleeps, otherwise he would have heard me knocking at the door.

The doors are deadbolted, but the upstairs window is open. Yanking a ladder out of Jenson's workshop, I pull the legs apart and plant it beneath the window. I come within ten feet of the window. I climb with unexpected agility. My head clears with each step. The fog of my tangled thoughts dissipates. The paralysis I have felt since my mother's death falls away. I must save my daughter.

I stand on the top of the ladder and reach up. My hand fully extended comes within a foot of the window sill. When I look down, I can see detail on the flowers, blades of grass separate from each other. My heart races, but my muscles are relaxed. I look up at the window. One jump with two possible outcomes. I picture myself crumpled on the concrete the ladder on top of me.

Then I hear it, the shrill, beautiful cry of my daughter.

I remember bending my knees to leap. I remember my hand wrapping around the sill, then slipping. My other hand gripping the trellis. I remember crawling inside, the wood of the windowsill scraping my belly, my head banging against Monique's wind up swing. And I remember how my feet thundering on the wooden floor down the hallway to her room.

He was there, leaning over her crib, a bulging canvas bag at his feet.

"Get away from her."

I remember picking up the musical lamp from the table. And stretching my arm back to swing at him—

This is real. I am five years old, and I sit on the painted horse of the carousel. My mother stands behind the metal fence, arms folded, the strap of her purse resting on her forearm. She smiles at me, but only the corners of her mouth turn up.

The merry go round jerks to a start. I crane my neck to keep my eyes on my mother until I can't see her anymore. In the half circle when she is out of my sight, the roses on my horse's mane blur, the music presses on my ears, and the up and down motion causes my stomach to churn. I feel dizzy. Colors swim around me.

The half circle when I cannot see my mother is too long.

I don't remember screaming only that I heard screaming and it must have come out of my mouth.

My mother is there. Her voice wraps around me like a blanket. I press my cheek against the rough wool of her coat and melt into her.

I hear her words as she strokes my hair, "Mommy is here. It's all right. It's all right. I'm right here, baby." I pull back, so I can see her face. The brown eyes with white specks, lips covered in orange lipstick, cooing soothing sounds. The face that tells me I am safe.

I grab Monique out of her crib and step over Mr. Jenson, lying on his stomach. He has a bloody spot on his head but his sides move in and out. My baby warms my arms and I hold her tight. "Mommy is here. It's all right. It's all right. I'm right here, baby." She stops flailing her arms, her chest moving up and down rhythmically.

And her eyes study my face.

M. Bennet Smith

THE DREAM OF JACOB DARLING

All these miles, men, lives, words –
a dream. All this time, a mystic vision.

We walk on the surface
of the earth, and listen to voices
as if we could believe.
Did you wait for Christ? I waited,
like waiting out a wasp, caught
in my hair. What did you see,

in the midst of your cocoon?
Wrappings of the world. If you remember,
you can show me out of mine. Did you
see where they brought Jacob up,
and where they laid him down again?
Did you see the blue-gray smoke
of cigarettes, hanging in the air? I saw
life in a fire, a dream in my hands.

Here is a message of hope
and half-glimpsed forms, stolen
from the sky: There is this silent
cricket, in the burning heart
of the world, waiting for peace.
There are dew-drenched morning
fields speaking to the wind.
There is Mary Dyer, walking on the air.

M. Bennet Smith

THE SECOND COMING AGAIN

A father and his boy are caught
in the middle of a firefight
in Bethlehem.
The boy is dead and the father
is bleeding. Behind them a wall

crumbles with each shot. Concrete
rains on them where they kneel.
All the gods of all our fathers
are helpless.

Palestinian radio repeats
in Hebrew,
Our children's
blood is as red
as your children's.

Maybe it is.

Maybe this will trigger
something in the brain
of someone responsible.

Maybe this will go on
until all that's left are echoes
of echoes
of the screams of bleeding
children.

Somewhere in England
a small bird rises, flies
through grime and rain,
is cleansed. It flies on
and through
and lights on a lake somewhere
in middle Africa.

The boy is still dead.

Lianne Elizabeth Mercer

CARDINAL SONG

Driving Texas Highway 39, I come upon two sheep nibbling road-side grass. Bleating, they leap for cover as I pass. Along fence rows purple thistles are dying, their fuzzy white heads drooping onto barbed wire. Buzzards lift themselves from a deer carcass to sit on fence posts hunched over like old men waiting in judgement. The wild roadside hums with the blessing of yellow May flowers. If we could forgive ourselves,

we might become buzzards abandoning rancid meat, climbing toward the sun, letting heat shrink our heavy blackness. We would feel our red heads melting across our bodies, and we would return to earth on flashing red wings, the only darkness remaining around eyes and beak not seeking reasons or words. Then, from groundsel and fire wheels, we might see the bloated deer rise, slim again, on wobbly fawn legs. We might hear ourselves singing lost lambs home.

Brent Short

CROSSING BOUNDARIES

It was in the middle of the story
where an unspeakable confusion reigned,
and the voice of mighty waters
spoke the crashing dark, a black enormity.
I was entering a different world
suspended between the old and new.
Not a bard among us, we rode on, impassively, mute.
Then language reemerged, shaped by the dumb communication
and needs (the feeding schedules) of all the ark's inhabitants;
both Man and beast were beneath
the late great world's contempt or pity,
irrelevant to its obsessions.
Who could destroy those whom God chooses to feed?
Pity became the source of all the other virtues,
arousing my pressed imagination.
Did you know there's a certain way horses drag
their hooves when a meal's required?
As this empathetic listening emerged,
so did the future, hidden as it is in the present.

Ready to venture out from my suffocating enclosure
(so solidly specified!), I stepped off
that reeking hulk onto a new place,
reconstituted, an approximation of the original.
Remembering the past proved problematic:
whole generations skipped over with no memory
of their having existed. Who could save
those whom God chooses to destroy?
My strange family drama paralleling
a wider-ranging cycle of pandemonium,
I made my peace with a world
offering no immediate assurance,
deconstructed by the roar—
a rainbow confirming regret as well as promise.

With a surge of judgment, the innocent
and guilty suffering equally,
everything uprooted dissolved, disappeared.
Rendered incurious again by the grape,
I was dreaming, a modest dream of
crossing fresh boundaries,
building a new world by simply understanding it,
conscious of being saved for what
I might be rather than what I was.
Living at the margins of ecstasy,
eager to speak many new languages,
my son, Ham, entered my tent,
crossing the threshold somewhere
between greeting and robbery,
forcing a door that was only half-open.
Reflecting on the mixture of blessing and curse
that is our expectation and disappointment,
and the mysterious ways the past is replayed,
I judged future implications by present choices,
and in the naming of it, I lost a son.

Janet Kaderli

JOYFUL NOISE

Lord, I see your creations
And I sing for joy at the work of your hands.
I step into the awesome majesty of nature
And I dance with my hands lifted in praise
                To the Holy One who created all things.

I, too, am your creation
Like the sandstone, the mountains, rivers, trees, flowers, lightning, and storm.
All your creations sing your praises,
Each in its own way.
I join the chorus of praise and thanksgiving,
My voice strong with joy, my steps and leaps like flight, my heart on fire with your
Spirit.
Holy, holy, holy! All power and glory and honor are yours forever and ever! The
thrust of the mountain into the sky, the surge of the tide, the flash of lightning, the
cymbal crash of thunder is praise lifted up to you.
I lift my arms as the wind of your Spirit washes over and around me, pushing me,
lifting me, 'til I feel I'm flying; lifted by you to take my place with the rejoicing of
your creations.
Glory to God in the highest! Glory to Jesus, your Son, our Savior, in whose name I
pray.

Janet Kelley

EPIPHANY

I.
Sister Mother Mary *"Ass*-rump-ta" was plain mean.
And I can prove it:

Onions in our Friday mac and cheese!
We knew they could have been
long and stringy enough
for alert! onion patrol
fingers to pick gross
stuff out. Oh no.
Everywhere
lurked carefully
cube-sized blocks
hidden inside dangerous
curves and buried deep in chalky cheese goo.

II.
Sr. Mother Mary Assumpta
would never guess:

I have kept pious for years
in vigilant search for

elusive onions.

Larry D. Thomas

STILL LIFE WITH OPEN BIBLE

(oil on canvas by Vincent van Gogh)

For pigment, he swirled his brush
in somber tones of green and brown,
rendering its binding
of heavy, cracked leather
strong as the foundation

of an edifice
built to house the heft
of Truth. Towering up
and angled slightly to the left,
loom four greenish rectangles

of Holy Scripture,
smudged with generations
of quavering fingertips
yearning for epiphany.
Into a background

black as the maw of night,
stuck in the socket
of a sturdy, metal candlestick,
juts the stub of an unlit candle
pregnant with the promise of Light.

Larry D. Thomas

CHURCH ORGANIST

Against a backdrop of sunset, the chollas
jut into the sky like clusters of old

rugged crosses. As she's done each rainless
evening since her retirement, she takes her place

in her porch rocker, pulls down her lower lip,
packs with a flat wooden spoon a dip

of snuff, and starts rocking. Notes of "Amazing
Grace," the last hymn she played before conceding

to the narrowing angles of arthritis,
swirl in her memories like dust

in a shaft of sunlight. She bends
her good ear to the wind,

straining to hear, drawing ever closer,
the names from the roll up yonder.

L. L. Ollivier

A LITTLE TRACT

He says the world's changed
its face, the trees
that bore the sky up once

a clacking of dry sticks,
the sky a blank eye
rolled back in a junkie's head,
earth a rag, the city
a persistent, idiotic

stammering. How could he imagine
the simple heart
of trees, the roots
of cottonwoods and poplars true

to water, the leaves
those trees will gather once the season
turns? How could he believe
a man would give his life up
willingly to heal the world's hurts, who can't
believe the trees, the easter
of their greening, their rising

from each driven nail, each wound,
their gathering in early light
shy as young deer
come to feed at morning's hand?

L. L. Ollivier

WILD MUSTARD

A little sun on water. Wind stippling
the Jeffrey pines. Geese carrying on
what I imagine must be
a congress on the qualities
of late winter days. Who knows

how long I'll have to listen
as pines bear rumor of storms
to come, as small birds natter
toward spring? Not every seed sown

will see the reaping. The kingdom,
Jesus said, is like the wild mustard
that full-blown spreads its bright
ineradicable blaze over miles. And I,
common fool, harrowing winter
for any breath or bloom of yellow.

Leona Welch

DEAR GOD –

I seem to be having a problem with Faith these days, like,
why should I believe in man's God when I'm not sure if
what I believe could be called anything other than my own
self-serving thoughts, of which I am my own master. [I think]

A Supreme Being, yes. Perhaps someone who must be above
the other gods. But, who's to believe one god created man in
his own image, then some man writes that God made woman
from a rib of man. [That book is not woman friendly!]
And she, to this day, is blamed for all his faults.
And for heaven's sake . . . why apples?

An ongoing problem has been the men in my life –
they don't seem to stick around for the long haul.
Father never said he didn't love me; he never said he did, either.
But then, he was never around until I was grown.
And I'm not the loser, and he's in his grave,
and I don't miss what I never had.

I also want to say I cannot respect any front-row preacher
who challenges a woman's choice, or not, to deliver another
fragile life. Adam certainly didn't rise at ungodly hours
to warm a bottle or change a diaper –
but now I think of it, neither did Jim, who played God
hoping to rule his kingdom. So, I wrote my own rules,
leaving out the part of treating him as a god, then leaving him
to survey what he no longer had. God what a mess!

Grandfather grew old with cancer [never smoked a day]
despite efforts to keep him forever young in my mind –
My son died young
and I'm told it's all part of God's plan
and I'm to worship one who would break my heart . . .
Don't even go there!

It's a God thing, you know –
bound in childhood to a religion decided by elders;
if it didn't happen in church, I couldn't go.
Believe by Faith, I'm told –

first I do: brainwashed works for me
then I don't: teenager rebelling against all authority
then, I just wasn't sure, because the hereafter seemed
to have arrived and hell was just outside the front door.

When I look at the nature of things and earth's beauty
all around me, I know there is a power beyond greatness –
when I take pen in hand, calming an inner turmoil,
or, hold a grandchild in my arms, I know peace and
am thankful for One who is loving and just;
forgiving all my doubts.

Thanks for listening and letting me sound off today.
I hope you aren't too disappointed in this rib.
I really have planted the mustard seed you gave me,
and I'm sorry for the crack about the apples.

Your loving daughter – Faith

Al Haley

THE BRIDGE

See how the arch spans
like a flexed muscle gaining
a grip upon the slow flow
of brackish water and dead
leaf eddies. The cage of old
rusted steel smells like the dented
cans buried back in the ash pit.

Good enough. I'll close eyes.
I will walk.

Creakings come from underfoot
along with the quiver and twang
of cable. Deep in the galvanized
guts, a six-inch rivet groans.
It is the link that cannot hold.

Reaction? I could jump,
making a splash below.

In warm shadows
cotton mouths hang motionless.
They speak velvet advertisements:
"It will not hurt, not at all."

No. There must be.
Other options.

Like going back, belly crawling,
hand over hand, clutching, shivering,
shakily reclaiming each inch
that leads home, to the kitchen
without the loaf of bread,
the cellar down to the last bottle of wine.

Now I bite
my lip. I ponder.

Eyes open wider, I focus
on the other side.

Such a holy sight.
It stuns the mind into silence.
Yes. There is. The other side.
The place of ten thousand brilliant
reasons, flashing in the light.
Each singing why I stake my life
on this faulty bridge.

Al Haley

IN BED WITH THE MYSTICS

It's you, luxuriating this a.m.,
stretching the long muscles and defeating
the night that shrank arms and legs
to less than standard length.
It's no one else but you, good ol' realist
you, fetching a fat glass of orange juice
with its vitamins and foaming promises
of sunshine induced health. It's routine,
correct? As are puckered carpet slippers
scuffing to the front door to bend down
and retrieve 110 pages of worldly woes
pressed into newsprint.

      The light.

Drop the fluid,
abandon all pictures and text.
An unintentional fast for your body and mind
sets in. As the world shuts down and punches
OFF and goes inside. You occupy a very small
place now, austerely furnished with a chair,
a window, a view of—

      The light.

Yes, they find you an hour later
(which you'll swear felt like five minutes)
sitting on the stoop, hands hugging domes of knees,
staring out at the navel's eye of dawn.
What happened, good sir or madam? Did you pass out?
How do you explain? That it was an unexpected
passing through. Soundless, thoughtless, without
feelings, just a joining and a being.
Wasn't pleasant, wasn't torture.
Simply *was*. A removal of heavy personality
and concrete cares to make a space
for the divine exercise, the weightless way
of John and Julian. A falling feather's
airy experience of God.

      The light.

Al Haley

FOR THE HERODS

Come morning, a deep silence
removes the trampling hooves
that have thundered past.
The dust of fallen houses settles
like soft snowfall on northern hills.
Smoke drifts sky-high from the ruins
while the spoor of men-beasts
lies thick in these streets.

In a rush, despair rolls
the large stone into place
and seals the results for a lifetime:
"Evil did fall on the land
and kill the most innocent."

It is dark and phantom
inside the cave of history
when the Herods
seem to have prevailed.
A rat nibbles the edge
of a granite shadow.

How hard to release the lament then
when the mind wants to surrender
to consuming fire.
Unnoticed, each martyr slips
away to self-immolate.
Yet the blaze of bones
casts insufficient light to see.

The last broken body.

Hold it. Feel it.
More quiet than stone,
the collapsed and pilloried flesh
dampens my encircling arms.
How wet.
To the dead, the living,
and the one called God.
At dawn I feel it soaking through.
It is him, of Him, from Him.
Such a fluid thing, this love.

H. Palmer Hall

THE VIGIL

We went to Easter Vigil, no longer an all night thing
only a brief hour and a half, the moon hanging bright
in a clear night sky, the fire flaring upwards to signify

what is now an old mystery. The priest sang, pure tenor,
words that have been sung and spoken for a thousand years
and we walked across a dark green lawn to the chapel.

Easter seduces with the season, brings us to a place
we do not want to be to celebrate a kind of birth
after death, whispers to us, to take and eat, to give

in to what cannot be readily believed, only accepted
with the bread and wine—a sense of community among
strangers who hold hands and sing of some shadowed thing

that will not be understood. At midnight, the vigil over
that once lasted and sang until dawn, we drove home
and talked of this and that. Easter had come in the dark

lit only by candles that mimicked the stars, a drooping moon,
a priest under a suspended cross, a sharing of flesh and blood
and the clattering sound of hands shaking a thousand bells.

Fredrick Zydek

LIGHT THAT IS MORE THAN LIGHT

The kingdom within
is the kingdom without.
Light that is more than light
takes all kinds of form.
Diversity is its middle name.

It wanders in every sparrow
and in the leaves of trees,
washes up on a million shores,
pirouettes in the ballet
of the seasons, glistens

in the roots of things, waits
for what silence knows
in every pebble and stone,
and drifts in the winds
that fill us like balloons.

It is everywhere delicious,
ready and willing,
reason and why, lovely
to contemplate and raw
as a baby's first cry.

Fredrick Zydek

THIS IS NOT A PRAYER

This is not a prayer. It's a bit
of undigested anguish rumbling
towards the great celestial gut,
optimism and panic thrown like
a javelin into a sovereign mystery.

This is not even a meditation.
It's a prodigal of phrases trying
to remember its own prodigious
acts of amazement, a contemplative
acrobat flying without a net.

This is neither a supplication nor a
plea. It is an adventure of the will,
an audacity whittled from awe
and suspicion, a string of curiosities
rumbling questions like apples

falling from Eden's tree. This is not
a prayer. It's a way of savoring
what the glands know but will not
tell, a vessel in which to pour
the red wine of wonder and doubt.

Mike Lythgoe

LOST ALONG HARMONY WAY

Leaving Interstate 64 is good for the soul.
Follow scenic routes in Southern Indiana,
Missing the right turn, lost well below

Little Egypt, Cairo, Illinois, where oil wells
Bob like large black birds,
Pecking—the cornfields' endless drills.

Bituminous crows pump, deliver
The earth's ooze, squeezing fossil fuel
From the soil along the Wabash River,

Hoosier state line. Van Gogh's gold,
Fertile soil, wheat, and corn waist high,
Yellow cut pasture, mowed hay rolled.

New Harmony—utopia—in Raintree County,
Fountain shaped for Orpheus's lyre; musical
Waters lost in a "rope walk" maze—not easy,

This center of the Harmonists' 19th century
Labyrinth—like Chartres Cathedral—a maze
Of patterns, pathways leading to eternity,

The earth's center, dead-ends, turns. Stop.
Listen. Go back. Reflect in the center,
Let someone pass, make a mistake, opt

Out, walk on to Read Rilke's Advice
To a Young Poet. Trappist monk, Thomas Merton's
Words on a Roofless Church, a meditation space—

No traditional buildings. Merton reminds us
Religion is not the past, not then—but now,
Here. The Prophet, Jeremiah, says to us:

We are like the clay
In the Potter's hands,
New Harmony's ways,

Circling, lives orbit on a potter's wheel,
Reflections on a sculpture: Angel
Of Harmony. Art enables us to feel

Harmony in St. Louis Cathedral Basilica
Before crossing the Mississippi.
Stay off I-64—Poseyville, Cynthiana,

St. Joe, Indiana, Mesker Park Road,
Evansville. At St. Joseph Cemetery, another
Sculpture, another angel in the road,

Up the hill, turn on St. John's Drive, scan
The Indiana limestone for a family name,
Find your mother's relatives if you can.

Get lost at 3 in the afternoon,
Scanning headstones on 3 June, seeking
Gravestones on a Sunday afternoon.

Lost. Remember the last view—
Holes open under tents, caskets
Made by monks. It was June, you

Recall, a burial four years ago;
A faucet near an ancient elm.
A November burial nine year ago.

Widows water cut flowers alone.
Lamey is wrong. No graves marked,
No father, no mother, a wife's stone

Is unknown, as is her husband's, Despair
In a garden of headstones, leaving—
Then a glimpse—Catherine's name—aware

At the eye's corner—Hugh cut into stone. Lemme
Anchors them side by side. Harmony
Is two graves found in the garden, not Lamey.

Harmony is lying face down
Where parental graves are found,
Relieved to find the sacred ground,

To pray for the repose of their souls.
Old Main Street home came down
For a parking lot, empty space in Ohio

River town. Leave absence east on the interstate,
Another wrong turn, double back to Archabbey,
Traffic is distracting, hard to concentrate.

On the high ground, above German farmers:
The seminary. Lost traveler hears the bells
Calling the Benedictines to vespers.

St. Meinrad's bells count the hours,
Call out at three quarters
Past the four o'clock hour.

The way to vespers is the way
Of work, prayerful hours, and penance;
Daily hospitality is the way of the Archabbey.

The black robes enter the holy place
At five in the afternoon,
Like black bulls to a sacrificial space—

Open ring—without defiance. Chapel space
Fills with their slow procession;
Chanting fills the hour with grace:

Hymns, psalms, alleluias, absence.
Archabbey of Indiana limestone
Offers renewal: music, ritual, silence.

Prayer is the center of the circle—
Where peace finds the Harmonists
As the travelers travel the circle.

Some will see the graceful limestone
Worked as a way in and out. See
How limestone turns to a headstone,

The right turns, a restful stop. We learn
To call the gift of finding the right way,
Grace. Others wander looking for a turn

Of luck, lost on Harmony Way. In dejection,
We the living lie down on the dead. We have lived
Holding a dying dog down for the injection.

The retriever died with open eyes, loving,
Beloved, labored breathing heart-stopped.
The living remember the missing,

Hugging warm fur, giving up the ghost.
Love is lost longing for a redemption.
A loving beast is lost. Our ghosts

Leave life on scenic routes, at interstate-speeds,
Changing lanes. One gets lost walking
In battlefields, wishing the darkest deeds

Undone. Earth is no utopia, yet we embrace the dirt.
Dust to dust we pray. Hi Meadow is an inferno.
Bobcat Gulch burned. Ashes scatter; blessed be the soot.

Ted L. Estess

BECOMING PART OF A STORY

Late in the day Barrett and I row down to the deep water at the end of Sun Valley Lake. He wants to try a new lure called a *Mepps*. He's twelve years old this summer and always looking for new ways to catch a fish. To his amazement, the Mepps no more than touches the water when a big Rainbow hits it.

We move around the lake for a couple more hours and Barrett tosses that Mepps out another two hundred times, but he never gets another strike. He is puzzled. How is it that he catches a trout on the first cast and never touches another the rest of the day?

To a considerable extent, it's a fortuitous matter, catching a fish. The fisherman only helps good fortune along; he wants at least not to get in the way. Some folks can't stand that about fishing, so they give it up.

All this reminds me of the series of events that led me to Houston, Texas, twenty-five years ago. It began when I answered the phone in Missoula, Montana. The voice said, "This is Donald Lutz from the University of Houston." I had never heard of Lutz, never thought of the University of Houston.

"I'm calling to invite you to be a consultant for us. Gerald Hinkle recommended you."

I started to ask, "What's a consultant?" And I didn't tell Lutz I wouldn't have known Gerald Hinkle if he walked in the door.

Later, I recalled meeting Hinkle at a conference in Williamsburg, Virginia. We ended up going out to dinner together. I wanted to try the peanut soup at Aunt Sally's Tavern.

I've met lots of people at lots of meetings, but this one time in Virginia I meet Hinkle; and two years later Hinkle meets Lutz at a meeting in Arkansas; and then a year after that Lutz calls me in Montana, thereby setting in motion a series of events that led to my moving to Texas. My intersecting Hinkle in Virginia and then his intersecting Lutz in Arkansas were at least as improbable as Barrett's Mepps landing right on top of that trout in the deep water of Sun Valley Lake.

Had I decided to eat a hamburger alone at Wendy's instead of going after that god-awful peanut soup at Aunt Sally's Tavern, my life in Houston, Texas, never would have happened. Twenty-five years of life in Houston would have been . . . well, it would have been nothing. Not a thing.

Now somebody might say, "That's just the way life is, Estess. What's the big deal?"

Well, to Estess, it *is* a big deal. It's my life I'm talking about, and I don't like thinking that my life, *as I have lived it,* may never have been. If it may never have been, it somehow seems flimsy, shadowy, inconsequential. I've heard that song about life being but a vapor in mid-summer's day and all that, but somehow I want *my* life to be more substantial, more solid. If it's not, the game doesn't seem worth the candle, and why am I spending all this time thinking about it?

A book arrived in yesterday's mail, a gift from my friend John Smith. The inscription says: *Ted & Barrett, drop everything & read this book. John.* I tend to do what I'm told, so last night I started reading *All the Pretty Horses* by Cormac McCarthy and came quickly to like John Grady Cole and Lacey Rawlins, two young cowboys living around San Angelo, Texas. One night John Grady and Rawlins lie down on a blacktop road to watch the stars:

Rawlins propped the heel of one boot atop the top of the other.

As if to pace off the heavens. [He said,] My daddy run off from home when he was fifteen. Otherwise I'd of been born in Alabama.

[John Grady said,] You wouldnt of been born at all.

What makes you say that?

Cause your mama's from San Angelo and he never would of met her.

He'd of met somebody.

So would she.

So?

So you wouldnt of been born.

I dont see why you say that. I'd of been born somewheres.

How?

Well why not?

If your mama had a baby with her other husband and your daddy had one with his other wife which one would you be?

I wouldn't be neither one of em.

That's right.

Rawlins lay watching the stars. After a while he said: I could still be born. I might look different or somethin. If God wanted me to be born I'd be born.

And if He didnt you wouldnt.

You're makin my goddamn head hurt.

I know it. I'm makin my own.

Some years ago, I made *my* goddamn head hurt trying to get through a big book by Jean Paul Sartre called *Being and Nothingness*. Like most folks who tried, I never made it, but I caught the drift. Sartre uses the French words *de trop* to capture something of what John Grady Cole is talking about. An occurrence—like Lacey Rawlins' getting born in Texas—is *de trop* if it has this accidental, fortuitous quality. *Contingent* is another word philosophers use to talk about the same thing. An occurrence is contingent if it may just as well have happened as not. An occurrence—indeed, a life—that depends so thoroughly on the unlikely intersection of Estess and Hinkle in Aunt Sally's Tavern is thoroughly contingent. It is *de trop*. And thinking about that makes my head hurt.

Now some folks are different from me. When they see how chancy life is, they're ready to have a go at it. They enjoy taking chances as long as they have a chance to take chances.

Others are like Sartre. They try to face up to the contingency and even to the absurdity of their choice—like my choosing to try the peanut soup at Aunt Sally's Tavern.

But for the life of me, I've never been able to respond like that, and I tell you why: I wasn't raised that way.

Now philosophers may scoff at this, but it's the only refutation—if I may use the word—to Sartre I've ever come up with. When he says that my life—thoroughly contingent because it is so thoroughly dependent upon the improbable intersection of Estess and Hinkle at Aunt Sally's tavern and then of Hinkle and Lutz in Arkansas—is as insubstantial as vapor floating off a lake, then I just have to say: I wasn't raised to think that way.

But I have to confess that my life felt mighty vaporous, mighty *de troppy* in the long months after I moved to Texas. I felt that I may as well be—or not be—somewhere else. It was as though I was somewhere I wasn't supposed to be, living a life I wasn't supposed to be living.

"That's why," I said to Michael one day, "I feel so bad." Michael was a therapist-friend who helped me out quite a bit during those long months.

"What's why?" Michael asked.

"Why I feel so bad moving to Houston."

"Last week you told me you didn't think you would ever figure it out."

"That was last week," I said.

"Well?"

"I feel bad because it's all an accident, my even being in Houston, Texas. It may just as well not have happened. None of it."

"That's curious," he said, and he started laughing. I don't know why, but his laughing got me to giggling, too. Before I had a chance to say anything, Michael said, "Our time is up for today. But, Ted, there's another possibility."

"What's that?" I asked.

"Instead of feeling bad you could feel good."

I said, "I doubt it."

Out here in Colorado this summer I've taken to rereading some old books. This week I'm rereading Norman Maclean's *A River Runs Through It*. Strange to say, but John Smith sent this book to me fifteen years ago, and here this week he sends me another. Norman Maclean talks about his youth in Missoula, Montana:

> By the middle of that summer when I was seventeen I had yet to see myself become part of a story. I had as yet no notion that life every now and then becomes literature—not for long, of course, but long enough to be what we best remember, and often enough so that what we eventually come to mean by life are those moments when life, instead of going sideways, backwards, forward, or nowhere at all, lines out straight, tense and inevitable, with a complication, climax, and, given some luck, a purgation, as if life had been made and not [just] happened.

To tell the truth, that's the way I was raised to think of life. The Baptists did it to me. From the time I was knee high to a grasshopper, good-hearted preachers and widow women told me that Good God Almighty had nothing better to do than make a plan for my life. I thus came to expect my life to line out *straight, tense, and inevitable* and for all the parts of it to go together like parts of a well-made story.

At the same time, other good folks were saying, "Young, man, you can do anything you want to do, be anything you want to be." In other words, I was to make up my life. But while I was trying to make it up, it felt like my life was going *sideways, backwards, forwards, or nowhere at all.*

Now this is a strange, even contradictory situation to be in: to be hearing, on the one hand, that somehow your life is planned even before you begin living it, and, on the other, to be hearing that your life is up for grabs. The first places you before one great Necessity; the other places you before an infinite number of possibilities.

To some extent what the Baptists said about life made me feel pretty good. After all, it was rather invigorating to think that Good God Almighty had a plan for little old Teddy Lynn Estess way down there in little old Tylertown, Mississippi. And that view made things pretty simple: all you have to do is figure out the plan and get on it.

The problem arose, of course, in the middle of life, when I saw that something so momentous as moving to the fair city of Houston, Texas, turned on so fragile a matter as a cup of peanut soup. I didn't seem to be living a life that had been made by the Maker of all life.

Nor did I seem to be living a life of my own making. It wasn't clear what story, if any, I was in; but it was clear that whatever was happening wasn't altogether of my own making. It was as though my life was being constructed out of fortuitous happenings and tortured choices, happenings and choices that could just as well have been otherwise or not been at all. Mine seemed a tenuous little life with no foundation at all.

"Michael," I said the next week, "I feel like I'm walking on thin air."

"That's the way I felt when I decided not to be a priest anymore."

"You were a priest? I didn't know that."

"For eighteen years. I even taught theology at a seminary for a while."

"Then you know what I'm talking about?"

"Maybe," he said. "Maybe you feel like you're walking on thin air because of a discrepancy. It's the discrepancy between a picture you have of life and the life you're living."

"How's that?"

"Well, the life you are living seems more fluid, risky, chancy than your picture of life allows, that's all. It's a common thing. Just change your picture of life and you remove the discrepancy. Maybe then you wouldn't feel so bad."

"But, Michael," I said, "don't you think there's something to what the Baptists said about—"

"Ted," he said, "I'm sorry to interrupt, but our time is up for today."

What I was getting ready to say when Michael called time on me was that maybe the old Baptist widow women weren't complete idiots in suggesting that one might live life as though it is made. Maybe one can see one's life that way. And wouldn't it be something to have both things at once: at the same time to acknowledge the fluidity and contingency in one's life, even to enjoy that, *and* to have the solidity and firmness that come from living a life that, in some sense, is made, where all the parts seem to fit.

"Michael," I said the next week, "I want both."

"Both what?"

"I want the old picture I had of life *and* to be truthful about feeling that my
life turns on chance."

"That's curious," he said. "I thought we decided last week that the discrepancy is painful. To remove the pain you have to remove the discrepancy, which means you have to give up that old picture of your life."

I said, "I don't want to give that up."

"That's not surprising," he said. "Still . . . ." And here Michael's sentence trailed off and silence took over for a while.

"Well," I said, "what are you thinking?"

"It's a possibility," he said.

"Really?"

"Really. But I still think you're making a mistake."

"What's that?"

"You want prospectively what you can only have retrospectively."

I wasn't sure I was understanding a thing the man was saying, so it made sense to ask, "What are you saying?"

"Just what I said. I mean that retrospectively—when you are looking back— life can acquire the kind of stability and firmness your old picture promised you. The story of your life can have a degree of stability and firmness, but I think you may have to wait a while for it."

"But is that the mistake?"

"No," he said. "The mistake is to expect prospectively what you can only have retrospectively. Prospectively, your life will continue to be fluid, chancy."

"That's bad," I said.

"There's another possibility."

I said, "I doubt it."

He said, "You may find it interesting or fun. You would have to practice, but you may."

"May what?"

"Find the chanciness of life interesting or just plain fun."

I said, "I doubt it."

"Like I said, you would have to practice."

"But," I asked, "what about that old Baptist picture?"

"That's not just Baptist, you know," Michael said. And then he took off talking about St. Augustine' *Confessions*. I almost interrupted to tell him that I was paying to talk to him not to listen to him talk to me. He went on to say that when Saint Augustine was forty-five or so, he wrote about how he got to be who he was. By that point his life had acquired a kind of inevitability about it. That's what gave him authority as a teacher. He felt as though his life could have been no other way, that his life was as it was from the very beginning.

I wanted to say, "That's what I want, Michael, and what I don't have and don't expect to have." But I didn't.

Then Michael said, "Whenever I taught Augustine to the seminarians, I asked them to memorize one line from *The Confessions*. The line goes like this: *sic curas unumquemque nostrum tamquam solum cures, et sic omnes tamquam singulos.*"

"Michael," I said, "Baptists don't speak Latin."

"Oh," he said, "I forgot." Then he started talking again, this time explaining that when Augustine wrote that line he was at a sufficient remove from certain events of his life that he could see how things fit together and that the line is speaking of God and that it expresses Augustine's sense of providential care in all things of his life, down to the tiniest detail.

"Michael," I said, "what does it mean?"

"Oh," he said, "it means, *He cares for every one of us as though he had no other for whom to care. He cares for all as he cares for each.*"

"That's curious," I said.

"Yes," he said, "it is."

Over the years I've thought a good deal about what my friend told me that day. In many ways, he was right: I was making a mistake. I sometimes still make it. The mistake is to expect always to feel that life is unfolding as it ought to unfold, as it has to unfold. To want too quickly for the pieces of life to cohere as in a well-wrought story.

I've tried to give it up, but I sometimes catch myself making the same mistake. Only now, I don't call it a mistake. I call it *my way of getting on.*

When you get past fifty years old—and perhaps before—you may at times see a pattern in life and see life lining out straight, tense, and inevitable. You may see your life becoming part of a story. And the story of your life may seem so stable that it feels as though it may well have been made in advance of your living it. Even those things that present themselves as so much sand blowing in the wind may seem, retrospectively, somehow inevitable. Without them, you would have missed part of the story and every part somehow seems necessary for the whole to be what it is.

But once you get past fifty years old, you've also had world and time enough to see why Saint Augustine would say *the soul is a great abyss,* even as he discerns providential care at every step. This great explorer of the abyss, then, fesses up to a deep-down and abiding ignorance about himself. Only in the shadow of such a confession could he—or my friend Michael, or anyone, for that matter—venture something so audacious, something so comically exuberant, as *He cares for everyone of us as though he had no other for whom to care.* He cares for all as he cares for each.

Tony Clark

ON CHRISTMAS DAY

This weather bodes well for hawks:
Cold, gray, with a thin mist
just a few degrees from ice,
and small creatures breaking cover,
deluded by midday darkness.

Last night at Christmas Vigil,
we took on our tongues the Body
and the Blood, in memory of Him.
Today we motor through rural Texas
committed to a necessary journey.

As we go, we watch the stalking hawks.
Some stand taut in skeletal trees,
some swoop low over ocher fields.
For predators, the body and the blood
bear strict corporeal definition.

Tony Clark

COMING TO TERMS WITH THE TRINITY

God in three persons, Blessed Trinity—
the magnitude of this Mystery
confounded my feeble belief.

The fault, I know, was my own—
a lack of grasp, or grace,
in my hard-shell perception.

Praise Father, Son, and Holy Ghost—
praise, yes, but comprehend?
There was the rub for likes of me.

The Father: Yahweh, Jehovah—
terror of my childhood
once sin became concrete:

Michaelangelo's stern finger-pointer,
wielder of the rod of retribution,
who rained down fire on Sodom

and Gomorrah, who raised the Flood,
tormented Job, put Abraham
to the unspeakable test.

And the Son: God made Man,
yet like no man before or since—
an alien all His earthly days.

An enigma even to those
who walked and talked with Him
on the dusty paths of Galilee.

He mounted his cross and died for us,
bought our paltry selves with blood—
can such perfection also be a peer?

But the Holy Ghost, who proceeds
from the Father and the Son—
here was a facet I could try to fathom:

Abstract, yet solid as the soul,
divinity both ephemeral and real,
imbuing every atom of creation.

When I hold in my mouth the thin,
sweet wafer of the Body, it is
this entity that nourishes,

that surges through my being,
penetrates my darkest places
and shores up my ramshackle faith.

G.C. Waldrep

CALVARY

Five p.m., taking the ramp onto the interstate I'm thinking
about the connection between fundamentalist Christianity
and bad architecture: say, the nouveau concrete-and-plexiglass
tower that rises one story above the faded Victorian clapboards
proclaiming CALVARY in four electric directions. Once
I thought the malady was confined to certain strains
of Lutherans and Pentecostals, which—however dissimilar
in theology—seemed to excel at the tasteless and banal;
but apparently this is a communicable disease. In a small
town south of here one staid church shingle—circa 1963—
advertises "contemporary worship" in day-glow letters
against black felt. I guess what moves me is the desperate
sincerity implied, the hand that pressed each letter,
newly-cracked from its plastic skeleton, into the narrow
space between the old fabric and the smeared glass.
I want to think of this as a noble gesture, even if the letters
came from Wal-Mart and the church secretary's father
still thinks the Klan was a good idea. Across the street
in the county office annex, the health department clerk—
full makeup, bleached hair—is saying "I can't, Mr. Wilson,
you know you need to come yourself, first thing
tomorrow morning," the voice on the other end of the line
buzzing angrily. Meanwhile I'm leaving Indy on a Greyhound bus,
headed for Ohio. It's April, the fields are greening,
there is in the air both a chill and that veritable intimation
of promise, of renewal. East of the city a large building,
wide and squat as a warehouse, is rising out of stubble.
The sign by the highway reads CATHEDRAL OF PRAISE.
It's ugly, and so is the truth about grace: the grey stones
the builders rejected, the lame and their ubiquitous prey.

G.C. Waldrep

DIES IRAE

When Lucifer fell on North Carolina
he came as a frost: past evening, that first moment
when the mind registers the day's closure,
the chill spreading against the final absence
of light in the west. He was like that,
settling in on the dark fields and small houses
before we understood the nature
of loss, before we even began to comprehend
the hard syntax of faith. Ever the grammarian
he kept us checking the true meanings of words,
testing the weight of each sentence.
There was torque. There was the elaborate
sprung architecture of our arguments,
our witty debates. Meanwhile the cold deepened.
We considered domestic emplacements.
Like thrown statues we stiffened into the postures
of a broken tongue, balancing impossibly, held steady
by will and by the thin ice, yet pricking.

G.C. Waldrep

IN THE BARN I HELPED BUILD

So much for the reach at evening, the ladder's rung
cold and wet to the palm's grasp, and the light
climbing too, thick-knuckled, into the haymow
and out through the streaked glass of the west window.
The loft is nearly empty in this season, only a dozen or so
bales of last year's hay wedged against the broad eaves,
and the loose underfoot like the yard dust into which
it is returning. Pegged into the far wall a pine shelf—
the builder's gesture toward order—above it nails
from which his tools hung. The window was a luxury,
so he could watch the sun sinking over his neighbor's
acre at day's close. He lives in Kentucky now.
No tools of mine hang from these nails; my own hands
are dumb to the workings of wood and all flesh; beneath me
the beasts snort at misplaced circumstance. But see
how the last glint strikes fire from the stock pond,
beyond the animal abrasions. Feel how the knees
bend, older, to the steel of one folding chair.

G.C. Waldrep

PRAYER FOR THE BITHYNIANS

Assist. If you do not
who will? In blood and testimony
our substance is spent, it is spent,
we love and are consumed
of our own affections.
Consider the lily: yes,

consider its pale bloom
in the brief interval before
it lies in the mower's wake;
likewise the birds, the mustard seed,
all proverbial inheritances
made tangible for our benefit.

For truly the instruments
are by their rhymes,
some slant, some distant
as in Dickinson or a symphony
by Ives—that disillusioned actuary
going door to door

with his distorted measures,
his church-house sentiment
Doppler-modulated,
his recollected faith.
Strait is the gate, and narrow
the streets of New England....

Assist, then. Calm the brass
and woodwinds, set the tympani
at peace with its musician.
Let the elm's bud insure
the consonance of our desire,
so late now, in this day.

Robert Wooten

JESUS'S SCRIBBLING

How interesting that Jesus scribbles in
the dirt. How interesting that no one asks
Him why. It does not seem to be a task,
but it apparently is not a sin.
Are there people who say that it was not
a wise use of thee time—scribbling—that it hurts
to think that Jesus scribbled in the dirt?—
no. There is evidence that they are hot
about the woman taken in adultery;
but in John 8:6 and 8:8 the scribbling
of Jesus happens without quibbling.
And He asks no one if they want to see.
Dirty writing is in The Holy Bible,
but no one turns it in and holds it liable.

Arthur Powers

FOR MY FELLOW POETS

"Why then should man, teasing the world for grace,
Spoil his salvation for a fierce miscreed?"
wrote Keats. And, colleagues, should you so need,
hold this page to the pale glow of his face

burning like a slow candle, the white lace
of his forehead, and the sandy weed
of hair, hanging, sweated and without seed,
to his cheeks. His eyes? His eyes stare at space

which is not space but that eternity
where art and fame and talent become toys
hardly fit to entertain small boys,
and even the body withers where it lies.

Greg Garrett

FREE BIRD

Free Bird is the story of a journey from despair to redemption. Clay Forester once had everything—or thought he did—but when his wife and son were killed in an accident, he wound up back in his old hometown in North Carolina going through the motions of life and trying to imagine how he might ever recover. When his birth father—missing since Clay was a baby—dies in New Mexico and Clay is prevailed upon to attend the funeral, he has to get outside his comfortable rut for the first time in years, and on the road he meets people who challenge him and—ultimately— change him to someone with faith enough to start over.

***

Here is how I woke on that Monday morning, the way in fact I always woke up in those days: by nine A.M., never later, someone started banging on the old upright piano downstairs in the parlor. There was no soothing prelude, none of that tuning you might get with an orchestra or two guys with guitars. Just thundering chords, then one, two, or three aging voices aimed my direction in gospel song. On that morning, it was Aunt Sister playing, and the song was "The Old Rugged Cross." I knew it was Aunt Sister by the rolling boogie-woogie left hand. She had not knowingly played boogie-woogie in fifty years, it being one of the bygone pleasures of her sinful youth, but nonetheless it got into her blood and still sneaked out where you might least expect it. Consequently, I liked her play better than the more formal chording of my mother and Aunt Ellen, although gospel piano is no humane way to wake up a man no matter who is doing it.

My name is Clay Forester, and in those days you did not have to know me very long or very well to see that I was a mess in just about every way a man could aspire to those depths. Even my stepfather, Ray Fontenot, who loved me as his own, used to drape an arm over my shoulder, draw me close, and tell me confidentially, "You know, son, you are a sorry excuse for a human being." I understand that this was his gruff way of expressing his love; I also know he was serious as a heart attack.

I used to be a lawyer like Ray, a pretty good one, in fact. But that was in the past. At the time I am telling you of, I played guitar and sang in a four-piece bar band called Briar Patch that played all over the Carolinas. The name came from the B'rer Rabbit story, I think. None of us could remember. Briar Patch was not even a very good band, which I had to admit to myself so that I didn't get delusions, as apparently I am genetically predisposed to do. We covered other people's tunes, mostly, things we all liked and I could sing: Springsteen, Roy Orbison, John Mellencamp, Tom Petty, the usual classic rock stuff. Some Stone Temple Pilots, Semi-Sonic, Vertical Horizon, Goo Goo Dolls for the youngsters. We aspired to ska, reggae, and our own songs, but hell, we'd been known to break out Elvis and Carl Perkins in venues where the crowd threw bottles, which happened more often than I'd like to admit. It's hard to be faithful to your art when you play in the kind of places where chairs break over men's skulls and women throw beer on each other and it's a virtual lock that one or more drunken hillbillies will start screaming "Free Bird, Free Bird" until you break down and play some Skynyrd.

Christ Almighty, I hate that song.

So that was my life. I once had larger aspirations, but about ten years before the time of which I speak, I suffered what I guess you'd call a personal setback, and I did not rebound from it. Or rather, I did rebound from it, but in wholly unexpected and unhealthy ways: back to my childhood home, to my old room, to a bizarre existence surrounded by old women who thought somehow that everyday life was a fitting excuse to sing praise.

Aunt Sister—Eula Mae was her given, but being she's the youngest, she grew up being called "Sister," and so there she was, sixty-some years old without a proper name to call her own—anyway, Aunt Sister switched over now to a rollicking "Onward Christian Soldiers," so I rolled out of bed, planting my feet on the floor with a reverberating thud so that the women could relax a little. They seemed to take the project of my continuing salvation seriously. Besides Aunt Sister, the women were my mother and Miss Ellen, the oldest and the scariest of the three. She was over seventy, but she still played piano at the Grace Tabernacle in Robbinsville. My mother played organ across from her most Sundays, except when she felt her life was being threatened by some new ailment, and on those occasions one of those Adams women from out Yellow Creek Road—not the ones on Talluah Road— would do their best to fill her heels. The week before, she had in fact been bedridden with colon cancer, although by Monday it was apparently far enough along into remission that she could join her sisters on the back porch to rock and shell peas and sip moisture-beaded Coca-Colas and act scandalized by my backsliding ways.

Don't misunderstand me. They were lovely Christian women, kind to children, generous to the poor and colored. But it is also true that they were capable of drawing and quartering a man with the silken strands of their words. My stepfather, Ray, in fact had moved out fourteen years before the time of which I speak, an act of sanity for which I admired him greatly, although he and my mother were still married and maintained a better relationship than most couples that I had known, my late wife and me included. He escaped; I stayed on in that household of women because I did not know where else to go, or how to live, or what to do with myself, because as I'm sure you recall, I was a sorry excuse for a human being.

I pulled on a Springsteen tour T-shirt, a pair of ratty Levi's, and my Birkenstocks, splashed some water on my face, then tramped clown-footed down the stairs so they couldn't pretend they didn't hear me and look up with badly acted surprise from some innocent conversation about my shortcomings.

"Morning," I called out as I entered the kitchen. I opened the fridge and spent a few minutes looking through it and ignoring the food already sitting at my place at the table.

"I made you some hotcakes," my mother said from the doorway to the parlor, her voice as soft as room-temperature butter. "I don't suppose they're any good now."

"Thanks, Momma," I managed to say, and I sat down to a lukewarm stack of buttermilk pancakes. She—Evvie Forester Fontenot—sat down across from me, and my eyes confirmed what my nose already knowed—that she had been to the beauty shop that morning for frost and curls. I cut and speared my first bite, poured a little more Aunt Jemima, and took another as Aunt Sister started up with ,"In the Garden." Miss Ellen was probably knitting: I heard her humming distractedly, then singing the end of each line before the two of them struck up the chorus in harmony, something like this:

Hmmmmm Hmmmmm alone
Hmmmmm Hmmmmm roses.

I chewed my aging pancakes reflectively. That was what my mother's love tasted like: sweet, sticky, and stale. Hard to swallow. It clogged my chest and sometimes made me gasp for air. I took a long glug of orange juice, sour now after the syrup, and then my mother cleared her throat, her opening to edged conversation.

"What time did you get in, Clay?" Momma asked without looking up from her hands—she had gotten her nails done too, but I could see she was not crazy about the color, peach or coral or some such thing.

"Late," I said. "We played our first night at a club in Charlotte, had to drive half the night to get back."

"What'd you make? I suppose it was enough to justify playing the Devil's music on the Lord's Day?"

"Five hundred. Split five ways, less gas, less stitches for Otis."

"Sweet Jesus preserve us," she said, although it was strictly pro forma alarm, since she did not bring her hand to her chest as she would for moments of genuine distress. "Where at this time?"

"Right smack in the middle of his forehead." I drew a line over my eyebrows with my finger. "Twelve stitches. He closes his eyes, he looks like a cyclops."

She couldn't help laughing, and she hated herself for it. She did not approve of my life, but she was ever a sucker for a punch line. That must have been how my father won her; I heard that he was a funny man, even if he wasn't worth a damn in any other respect.

"You ought not to keep a drummer around that can't stay clear of those kinds of things," she said, trying to stop laughing and be solemn and motherly. "That Otis is trouble. I've been telling you for years."

"Yes, ma'am." Twenty-five years, at least. I used to go over to Otis's house in fifth grade to spin records, the beginning of her long train of rock-and-roll resentment against Otis, although after his mother died when we were in seventh grade— and to her eternal credit, since my mother is a closet racist, and Otis is the blackest of my friends, from the top of his modified 'Fro to the bottom of his Lenny Kravitz conquistador boots—my mom used to take food over and take Otis out shopping every August for school clothes.

From the time we were fifteen Otis and I put together garage bands that played pizza parlors and private parties. And when we were seventeen we put together a band that played "Stairway to Heaven" and "Layla" at a church talent show in Asheville, a band that in fact was chased off the stage and all the way to the boys' restroom by a throng of shrieking junior high girls, like something out of Hard Day's

Night or something. What they would have done if they had caught us I will never know; all the same, I looked around daily for something that could compare to the surreal adrenaline rush of that moment.

Momma was waiting for my response, though, so I picked up in the present. "A good drummer is hard to come by. If he was just a bass player, now . . . "

She gave me an acidulous look of disapproval, but if she really knew me, she'd know that I didn't need to be lectured about alcohol and self-destruction. Since my personal setback, I hadn't so much as taken a swig of beer. When we were on stage, I sipped at a Dr. Pepper, and if I happened to see a fight brewing in front of us, I unplugged my guitar and just walked away.

There's enough pain and heartache in this life without having to go looking for it.

When I said earlier that Ray Fontenot was my daddy in all but name, I was alluding to some of that heartache, which starts early and, I suppose, doesn't let up until you die. Here it is, for what it's worth: My real father, Steve Forester, a.k.a. Steve Forrest, left us when I was still in diapers to try his luck in Hollywood. He couldn't get his car to start—it was a 1961 Triumph that Momma said he spent near as much time pushing as driving—and Momma was screaming at him and throwing things, so he abandoned it, boarded the bus to Asheville, and then headed west from there. The car was about all he left behind, and it was about as worthless as he was: Ray and I had been trying to get that car to run for nigh on ten years and nary a peep did we hear.

He never came back, but he did write us three letters, coinciding with his three major speaking parts. In the first, he wrote about how he thought he'd be able to bring us out there shortly. In the second, he said things were harder then he ever imagined. In the third, he didn't say much beyond he wished he'd never come. There wasn't a fourth letter that I know of. No one knew what happened to him after that, and after Momma had people look for him without any luck, she had to have him declared legally dead eight years later to marry Ray. He dropped out of sight, and sometimes even out of mind, if a missing father can ever truly be called missing. And then late one night I was watching that cable show, you know the one where the guy and his little robots make fun of bad movies, and lo, there it was: Mission to Mercury, his starring role, in all its B-movie glory. And there he was: my dad, the so-called Steve Forrest, a dimple-jawed Rock Hudson type done up in cheap spaceman duds. The pounding in my chest was a strange mixture of awe and embarrassment, something like Hamlet at last tracking down his daddy's ghost and finding him in a pair of Goodwill overalls.

"Momma," I called back into the house when he came on screen. "Momma, come quick." Within seconds, she ran down the hall toward me, slippers flopping, clutching her robe about her throat. "Is the house on fire?"

"It's Daddy," I said, and I pointed to the TV. "Isn't it?"

She squinted at the screen, padded right up to the set, dropped her hands to her sides, and shook her head like she couldn't believe it. "Yes, that is your daddy." She stood for a moment more before letting out a long breath. "My God, he looks silly. And what are those things at the bottom of the screen?"

"They're robots," I said. "They're making fun of Daddy. Apparently he was one of the worst actors in the history of . . . history, I guess."

"Clay Forester," she said, and she whirled on me, "if you can't say something nice about somebody I'd thank you to keep your mouth shut." She watched my father for another moment as he piloted his cardboard spacecraft toward strange and unknown lands. Then she started bawling, which brought the rest of the house to life just as the show went to commercial.

Miss Ellen, of course, was first to arrive and take stock of the situation. "Young man," she said, exhaling frost at me, "you should be ashamed."

"I am," I told her. "Pretty near all the time."

But then the show came back on and some order was restored, explanations tendered and accepted. We settled back to watch as my father made contact with the surprisingly shapely female inhabitants of Mercury, and on one of the commercial breaks, I heated up some microwave popcorn and passed it around. It seemed to be an occasion of some sort.

"He was a handsome man," Aunt Sister offered at length.

"He always was that," Miss Ellen said. "Although it's clear now he couldn't act his way out of a paper bag. Carousel gave him the big head, I suppose. He was awful good in that, but whatever made him think people would love him just as much in Hollywood, I will never know."

"I do not like those robots," my mother said, and that was the last I knew about my father until Ray called while I was sitting there that Monday morning eating pancakes.

"Your mother wants me to talk to you about something," he said, his voice apologetic. "Come for lunch?"

"Gladly," I said. "But Ray, my mother is less than four feet away from me." I put my hand over the receiver and leaned forward. "Momma, what do you want Ray to tell me?"

"Oh," she said, looking her nails over again, "this and that."

I stifled the urge to blaspheme, and instead released my most piteous sigh. Two could play that game. "All right, Ray. Barbecue?"

"You bet," he said. "See you in a few, son."

I hung up and tried without success to get my mother to meet my gaze. I never realized that fingernails could be of such all-consuming interest. My aunts were singing "I'll Fly Away," the second hand on the stove clock was moving in distinct and separate clicks, and at last she got up to clear my plate.

"Well," I said. "I guess I'll get around. Go see what the old man wants. I'm sure it's important."

She paused with her hands in the dishwater, looked over her shoulder, and delivered her usual parting: "Clay, you really ought to get married again. Settle down. Take up your work. Make a real life for yourself." There was a new urgency in her voice that morning, almost a tremble for some reason I couldn't fathom; I didn't perceive that I was noticeably more distressing or distressed that morning than in weeks, months, years past. Still, I'd reached the point where I just nodded my head in agreement when she said it, nodded because it was true, all true, everything she said, and I knew it the way I knew I ought to love my country, worship my God, support my local sheriff.

"Yes ma'am," I said softly. "I surely should." And I went off to find some clothes that a man could wear without embarrassing his stepfather.

Ray and I were always the only white customers in Dolly's, which was as it ought to be. The fewer white people the better; we'd just ruin it with Elvis knick-knacks and combo platters and plastic forks, the most useless utensil on God's green earth. Bobby Blue Bland and Muddy Waters were playing on the jukebox, and barbecue here was brisket so tender it fell apart in your mouth, served on wax paper with Wonder bread, onions, and sliced dill pickles. The sauce came in plastic cups, and it was as hot and sweet and musty as love in a backseat.

I'd eaten most of my food. We'd been making small talk on North Carolina basketball and other such essential topics, and I was beginning to eye the cherry cobbler when Ray cleared his throat. Unlike my mother, Ray never cleared his throat for pleasure, so I knew that either he was choking or this was truly serious business.

"Son, your mama got a telephone call last night from Santa Fe, New Mexico," he said, and he looked up from the table to watch how I would receive his news. "It's about your daddy."

All the meat I'd ingested became an iron lump in my stomach. "I hope to hell he doesn't think he's coming home after all this time," I said. "That train has left the station."

"No, son. He's dead. Died yesterday. The funeral's in New Mexico Friday."

Etta, our waitress, came over to see if we wanted cobbler, and I have to tell you, even with that bombshell dropped we nodded our heads at her. It was that kind of cobbler. "So I thought since you'd need to go to the funeral—"

"Like hell, Ray," I said, then caught myself. "That man in Santa Fe was no more my father than Etta here."

"And I sho ain't no man's father," she said, slapping our bowls of cherry cobbler down in front of us. And that's for certain; her bosom weighed more than my entire body.

"You're my father, Ray, the only one I've ever had. You took me in, you raised me, you did your best to make me a good man. I don't have a father in New Mexico. Case closed."

He smiled sadly in appreciation. "Still, son, the last thing that man did was ask for you. He made a mistake, sure, and it was a big one, but—"

"He should have thought of that a long time ago." I took a bite of that crust, golden and buttery and coated with the cherry filling. "He left his family. And he never cared what happened to us after he left. No Christmas cards. No birthday cards. No hey I'm still alive cards. Good riddance, I say. Tell me that he burned to a crisp in those wildfires around Los Alamos and I'll be a happy man."

B.B. King and Lucille took up "The Thrill Is Gone," and I closed my eyes and shook my head in time to the music. I didn't want to talk about it anymore.

"Damn, son, " Ray said after a verse and a chorus. "I can't believe you're making me say this."

I opened my eyes. His face was red as his cobbler. "Well, spit it out, old-timer," I said. "I'm a busy man."

He took a good look down at the table, rubbed at a spot of barbecue sauce there, cleared his throat. "Son, I don't believe in signs. You know that. It's a bone of contention between me and your momma, if you don't mind my saying so. Unlike some folks, God does not deign to speak to me in an audible voice and remind me to take out the trash. But yesterday, something happened."

I spooned my last bite, pushed my bowl away from me, arched an eyebrow, and waited. He looked up at me, his gaze dropped immediately, and he went on.

"I had some time on my hands last night, so I went out and put that head gasket on your daddy's car."

I nodded. "The one that came in last week. I still need to pay you for that."

"Yes, you do. But that's not what I want to tell you. I put the gasket on. I got everything tightened down. I hooked up the battery. And then I turned the key and she started."

I swallowed my last bite of cobbler and sat up straight. "You got the Triumph started?"

"I did. And she kept running. And started up again when I turned her off." He shook his head and pursed his lips, like he didn't know what to think. "We've been working on that car for ten years." He looked around, maybe to see if there was some way he didn't have to say this. "Son, don't you think it means something that last night of all nights, his car comes back to life?"

"You're scaring me now," I said. "Not with your haunted car story. But you are scaring me."

"It's got to mean something, son. Don't you think?"

I sat up straight and looked him in the eyes. "Ray, I don't care if that man's ghost walks in the door over there and starts singing 'Fever.'" Ray was a big fan of Peggy Lee. "He was not my father. You are. I'm not going to Santa Fe tonight, tomorrow, or ever. That whole damn state is on fire, anyway. Plus I've got a show tonight. And tomorrow night. And the next night. I couldn't go if I wanted to. Plus I don't want to. Can I be any more explicit?"

Ray sighed and shook his head. "No, son. I said what I came here to say. What you do with it is up to you."

"Thank you, Ray," I said, leaning across the table. "I know you mean well. And I know the Christian thing to do would be to forgive the bastard. But I'm not interested in doing the Christian thing."

He sighed, for this was a bone of contention between us. Ray was a good Christian and devout Southern Baptist, although not so devout that he felt personally led to boycott Disney, convert the Christ-killing Jews, or shove women out of the pulpit and make sure they were at home cooking for their husbands where they belonged. I felt bad, and I hung my head a little. "Listen, I gotta go. Otis is expecting me at two."

"All right, son. When do you want to pick up that car?"

I stood there for a second and then I shrugged. "Hell, Ray, I don't know. We can talk about it later, okay? Thanks for lunch."

"Always a pleasure," he said. He got up and hugged me, and damned if there wasn't just as much love in his eyes as before we sat down to talk. I guess fatherhood suits some.

He patted me three times on the shoulders when he hugged me, like he had since I was old enough to remember being hugged, then he sat back down, and as I walked out, he waved his good-bye, one finger raised like he still had one more thing to say.

He didn't think I saw him gesture to Etta for more cobbler as I shut the door. But I did.

Cleatus Rattan

GOODNESS KNOWS

She went her way. She'll find me later,
I thought. I walked straight as virtue
south with my almost useless 410 breached under my arm.
The deep meadow grass
waved me along with the northerly breeze.
Thinking to check the west fence,
I turned right
for 100 yards. Finding little
of value hiding in holes,
I followed my path
back to the original
rut.

On briefly south
then seeing a cross
through the narrow creek,
I came back,
trekked
east through the gushing water,
then up
the hill to sit, watch the sun
fall.

My collie came running
far below me
following
my scent. She was perfect:
south, west, then east to the pure water
where she lost me. She followed
the same route over and over
believing
she could find me.
I waved my crooked scepter,
but she could not see me.

Content
I watch her
invoke blessing after blessing.

Cleatus Rattan

TENDER MERCY

Almighty God
to whom all hearts are open,
I know thee.

You desire for me to know
beams that hold,
fires that warm,
water that purifies,
has strength to crush,
power to burn,
ability to extinguish.
No secrets are hid.

Cleanse my heart. I am
creation,
not extension.
There could be
no pleasure without me.
Your image I am.
I imperfectly love thee.

Cenotaph, poems by Eric Pankey. ISBN 0-375-40764-2. Alfred A. Knoph:New York, 2000. 85 pages, $22.00. Reviewed by Michael H. Lythgoe.

Before giving a poetry reading at RW Books, in Manassas, Virginia, Eric Pankey was interviewed by Jennifer Peltak, a local journalist. Reflecting on his childhood in Missouri, and how his writing has changed, Pankey said: "Growing up, there was so much yelling, it was good to not create a voice" (*The Daily Journal*, March 3, 2000, pp. A 12 & A9). Where Jeanne Murray Walker creates many voices from imagined ancestors, and immigrants moving west, creating their part of America, Susan McCaslin voices the personae of gospels: Mary, Martha, and the apostles interacting with Jesus (see reviews in *Windhover* 2000).
Not so with Pankey.
Eric Pankey's poems, in this third volume of a trilogy, are more meditations than poems alive with characters speaking in dramas. His poems pursue a presence, not a voice. *Cenotaph* is his fifth collection of poetry. His last three books are like panels of a triptych, linked, three parts of one piece of art conveying an emptiness of lost faith.
Like McCaslin, Pankey writes meditations. Her poems are meditations on the gospels. There is a great difference, however, in how each poet confronts the muse, the creative imagination, God, or the goddess of poetry. Each writer is aware of the "gift" of inspiration, but for Pankey the Muse is a stingy mistress, more about what is missing than what is generous and giving:

> I am yours as your shadow is yours,
> And when I withdraw at noon, or loom
>
> At sunset, distorted and torn by
> The stone arabesques, that is my habit
>
> And not an act of mischief or treachery.
> What name can I give you that you might hear
>
> And in hearing, turn, as if to your own voice
> Spoken from the sheltered dark of here and now?
> ("The Muse's Admonition")

What is missing is the key to this rich collection of poetry. In "Speculation and devotions," Pankey published some notes he made during the time he was composing the poems collected in *Cenotaph* (*Image*, number 26). One of his notations reads: "The imagination is a hooded falcon." This is a bird to be wary of, a dangerous thing, but a good hunter when tamed or trained. What is missing is not just the Muse, but frequently faith itself. The cenotaph giving title to this book conveys the emptiness of a monument marking a memory—a gravesite, if you will—but not the tomb itself. The remains are elsewhere, or everywhere—like the dust in the air. Such a perfect symbol for the art Pankey makes.

If Pankey does not sound a full range of voices, there are whispers, and sounds from gorgeous landscapes, internal musings, music. It is not yet clear that a Virginia landscape has been contained in Pankey's poetry. He has been living in Fairfax, Virginia, and teaching for a couple of years at George Mason University. The Muse seems to have whispered most from the Connecticut shore of tidal flats, and salt marshes, over several summers. This is the predominant landscape of his last two volumes, *Apocrapha* and *The Late Romances*. In this volume, it is the landscape informing "Cold Spring Brook"—a sonnet sequence, the second of seven parts in the book. Nature is the focus of these sonnets, and the flux, the changes in life, the seasons, life and death; the changing weather runs through these lovely poems like the tide's ebb and flow.

> He has made of the narrow threshold
> Between landscape and contemplation
> An unlit altar where he augurs,
> Where the thicket reads as a pathway,
> Dusk as the dross of molten metal,
> As blown smoke, driftwood's mineral ash,
> Where memory becomes desire
> Without alchemy or revelation,
> Without the sediment of regret....

This is the third of eight sonnets in the sequence. It is highly representative of Pankey's strengths. It offers religious imagery in a natural setting, lyrical sounds, and a fresh treatment of traditional form. But it also conveys a prayerful tone, almost liturgical, tolling out the elegiac hours. Something is still missing, unsaid. It is a feeling in the poet like tinder waiting to be lit, but "it will not catch" because the breeze is damp and the "jackstraw" is too wet and cold. There are no miracles in this poem, no alchemy, no revelation, no resolution. This is where *Cenotaph* leaves off: emptiness—beautiful—but empty. What is missing is the presence of religious faith. The landscape is pastoral here, in Cold Spring Brook, but not Eden. If "memory becomes desire," it is both the memory of a lost past we seek to recover, but also a faith felt once and then lost. The desire is to recover what is lost. We have all lost Paradise.

There are two other landscapes Pankey writes into his poetry: Italy and Missouri. The Italian imagery continues to add color and classical settings—literary, and historical—to Pankey's work. He grew up in Missouri. His early work is rooted in Missouri rivers and woods. Memories of his family and Missouri scenes are recovered again in this collection.

> My dreams are a child's dreams.
> I remember nothing but the waking,
> Let the maple drop its keys to the wind.
> Let the blue jay jimmy the morning's latch.
> Let each secret I have kept keep me safe,

O God of Clamor. O God of Silence.

("Nocturne and Morning Song")

These lines I take to be about the Missouri landscape, a landscape of the heart, as is "Confessional Poem," and "The Cold war." The last poem is a lament for his parents who both died of disease from smoking. He has made some peace with the spirits of his parents in these later poems. The eight poems in "Elegiac Variations," the fifth section in his collection, speak from both Missouri and Italian settings. In the third poem in this sequence, the moon keeps "its vow of silence," but shines on a pruning hook in a vineyard

> Left to rust in a furrow
> You follow your father home
> How can one not mistake
> Intensity for purity
> Paradise for these ill-lit shambles
>
> By now the dark fields are wild with rose
> And the thistle worn to a crown.
>   (3. "The Parable of the Vineyard")

Gardens have thorns; the poem seems to be alluding to the agony in the garden. The 6th and 7th and 8th variations offer more European landscape imagery, like Italy. There are olive trees and cypress trees, swallows, a lizard on an Etruscan wall—"still it holds its tongue." These poems are rich with tones from a painter's palette: "green and quicksilver in the sepia shadows." There are also marble ruins. The lines are painted with a delicate brush. The artist who writes these words is obsessed with portraying both detailed scenes on small canvases, and deep emotions, but in quiet, reverential tones. There are blues, charcoal sketches, 'sandstone, raw sienna, and native umber," icons, doves, pewter, and "pale honey." Colors and textures give Pankey's poetry an atmosphere suggesting life and nature are scenes in paintings: beautiful, silent pigments on a canvas, landscapes.

It is tempting to select more mysterious, musical lines from Pankey's work. So I commend the whole of this book to you, gentle reader. In rereading some of John Clare's poems recently, one finds lines like "I speak in low calm breathing whispers." There is also a poem beginning "black absence hides upon the past...." Carol Kizer's comments on Clare seem equally appropriate for Eric Pankey: "His true occupation was to wander the woods and fields, lying silent in the grass for hours on end, inspecting the busy insects, admiring the weeds, or keeping watch over a bird's nest, carefully noting the color and number of its eggs while awaiting the parent bird's return. These are the themes in Clare's poems that contemporary poets, if they are fortunate enough to know Clare's work love the best" (quoted from Kizer's Introduction to *The Essential Clare*, published by ECCO). Pankey has the focus on nature that Emerson showed in his writings, an attention to detail. But he also journeys into Christian realms. Pankey transcends the natural world. This ability to relate nature to the spiritual world marks the high quality of Pankey's poetry most admired by this reviewer. Yet his natural imagery is not only grounded in botany, or the strong, obsessive gaze into the great outdoors; his images also remind the reader of the Church. "It is not resemblance that compels, but difference we are asked to see as resemblance, that evokes disquiet and mystery (*Image* 26, p. 86).

In the end, Pankey writes his way toward the presence missing from the *Cenotaph*, reminding us there is hope in the empty tomb, the sign of the Resurrection. In another of the notations he published in *Image*, he ponders: "God as spirit: while it suggests immanence, it also suggests transience, a thing like salt in suspension, a dust moved about by wind. A permanent transience? Let that be our last word: Now you may have the final word" (7. "Nocturne and Refrain" p. 61).

Slow Dance On Stilts. **Poems by Marie Jordan, LaJolla Poets Press, La Jolla, California, 2001, 80 pages paper, $11.00. Reviewed by Paul Stangeland.**

Slow Dance On Stilts is the title of the new book of poetry by Marie Jordan, a writer's writer who teaches writing to enthusiastic classes at Mira Costa College in Oceanside, California and is also popular on the guest lecture circuit, speaking often at colleges and universities throughout the country. Something that Jordan does not advertise, but which tells in her work, is her passion for art, per se, especially modern and contemporary art.

Slow Dance On Stilts could, indeed, be explained as the frisson between Jordan's artistic sensibilities and the desire to compress her experience into language using a working writer's discipline. The result is a montage stemming from honed, mature senses, and characters who blur traditional boundaries between 'self' and "other." Jordan consistently gets up to meet life more than half way with a hunger that does not get satisfied and stop.

The poems in this book are broadly exoteric, which is to say both worldly and grounded, and Jordan's vocabulary is rich with natural detail. Each poem is crowded with multi-dimensional images and impressions, and her vivid, even fantastical descriptions create a mood in which one arrives at her perspective unconsciously as her poems are read. With writerly wit and an artist's eye, Jordan paints with words a myriad world that evolves with or without our understanding or acceptance. She is wry without cynicism, rarely sentimental, and she longs to fit with the subtle yet pervasive rhythms and cycles of nature that alternately illustrate and instruct her perception and interaction. These are poems that concern Nature as part of the human experience, and the human condition as reflected in nature. Regardless of the setting, the natural world is never far away, even when the landscape is urban, or personal.

Veteran poetry editor Kathleen Iddings must be given at least some credit for the book's narrative shape. The book begins with "The Cutting Down of All My Trees," wherein young men ooze desire as they ravish the hillside behind Jordan's home. The book closes with "When They Come For Me," an oddly compelling mix of an elegy for the self and a passionate promise to stay in the hunt and open to whole experience in the end. The poems between these bookends are layered with the literal and the abstract, metaphor and metonym, and there are gemlike allusions and references for readers to discover. Throughout, Jordan retains a very personal perspective that she unabashedly opens up for and shares with her readers.

It might be said that *Slow Dance On Stilts* owes a debt to Sylvia Plath. Like Plath, Jordan is unstinting in a way that bespeaks true *Sturm und Drang*; yet Jordan is withal a survivor. And whereas Plath's humor is ever dark and cutting, Jordan gives over to mirth as part of an ongoing cycle of affirmation. In fact, Jordan goes confessional poetry one better, being one who understands and accepts her own role as agent and creator of her experience, not one who refuses to disempower either the agency or the experience itself. These poems are charged with a certain breathless, edgy quality that creates little fissures, nooks and crannies that beg the reader to return for a closer look. Consider the following:

From "Island Artist":

> Akalem paints her house
> with grass brushes
> and blood-red pigment,
> her palms, flat like wood,
> work the mud and cow dung,
> fingers, tough as rivers
> leave a black and white snake
> coiled on the wall
> with the yellow stripes running
> thick and fast as though being chased,
> the earth meeting itself ...

From: "Thundering Tigers":

> The air is webbed, woven in steam,
> tight hot threads of air flume around the heads
> of the travelers, swamp enters their boots,
> peels the polish off the lady's toes ...

From: "In Search of Verbs":

> You recall the man who ate his continental
> breakfast danish at the corner table,
> how he sniffed, swallowed, gulped
> with such vigor — a man
> of a thousand verbs. It's yesterday
> you searched for, you're not
> finished with the fiction
> of things past, the who of you
> beneath the ribs, the one
> you've tried so hard to reinvent.

The poetry in *Slow Dance On Stilts* as a whole succeeds in establishing and maintaining the proper tone and mood. I highly recommend this book.

The Drowned City, poems by Jennifer Atkinson. ISBN: 1-55553-454-6. Northeastern University Press: Boston MA, 2000. 83 pages, $9.00. Reviewed by Michael H. Lythgoe.

Jennifer Atkinson's second book of poems won the 2000 Morse Poetry Prize. Carl Phillips selected *The Drowned City* as the winning collection. In his introduction, Phillips writes that Atkinson's poems attempt to answer questions of belief faced with "staggering indifference." If faith is an absence, something missing, or rather unanswered in the poems of Eric Pankey, here faith in divinity is a sunken ruin, a drowned city to be visited, if not recovered.

This collection is distinguished by sensuous language. Atkinson's lines are well wrought, often musical, and finely crafted. Her imagery unfolds from the natural world. She is a close observer of fields, streams, birds, and shorelines. Her poems are frequently meditations informed by biblical references, memories of loss, Church history, a mother's love.

There is a first person's voice in many of the poems, but most speak distantly from a third person. There is a narrative style frequently describing a brief moment in time, a sense of place, emotions recounted from an event, or a visit, or a memory— but few actual story poems. An exception is the poem, "What Happened Next":

> It's not long before the things of this world
> revert to story and symbol

Here, a voice speaks from the East, seemingly set in Tibet. It proceeds with a tale of Buddha and the king cobra.

> I don't remember what happened next
> —lightning and thunder, flash and voice.
> ...Joy might last
> that long, as long as the silence between
> illumination and when its echo catches up.

"What Happened Next" reveals several of Atkinson's poetic characteristics. She is sensitive to sound and sense, flash and voice. She uses the image of fire frequently. She is subtle in weaving in references to other poets (here Rexroth's *One Hundred* refers to his poems in translation, ancient Chinese verse). She also places Eve in the story, not just Buddha; and the serpent in paradise is not so much the devil as an intelligent snake the woman meets "eye to eye...engaging its intelligence." A mysterious passage, but such a style gives much pleasure, as do her fresh reflections on "the end of suffering." She writes, "Nobody suffers—yet"— meaning the serpent in the garden has yet to succeed in getting Adam and eve to sin. In fact, Eve is present without Adam.

These poems are also collections, words conveying mixed media, actual constructions of paint, pictures, cloth materials—pieced together in layers like a collage: "Three Years: A Composition/In Gesso and Graphite," and "The Chester-

Hadlyme Ferry: A Composition in Graphite, Crayon, and a Line (in English) of Montale." There are other Italian references besides the Italian poet Montale. Her landscapes are the seashore and marshes of her Connecticut youth, and Cannaregio, grape arbors, palazzos, scalded sands, cold seas.

The sea runs through this book literally from "drowned marshy islands" to "surf-broken wharves." She dreams

> ...of rescue, as if I'd been kidnapped and held for
> ransom.
> As if rescue meant salvage from solitude, that wide salt, scalding
> cold sea.
> ("Sundial Ghazal")

This reviewer admires Atkinson's gifts of internal rhyme and alliteration, her allusions to Father Gerard Manley Hopkins, S.J., and Hart Crane.

Her book's title and use of the ghazal form for the final section suggests the works of Adrienne Rich also influence her writing. Rich published a collection of poems called *Diving into the Wreck*. Early in her career, Rich also published a series of "Blue Ghazals." Atkinson uses the ghazal form loosely to compose a series of poems in couplets of ten lines each, without Persian or Urdu references.

Jennifer Atkinson's religious imagery in *The Drowned City* is liturgical and biblical, architectural and artistic. Her poems refer to saints' days, "The Feast of the Assumption," and nuns' habits, bell towers, spires, stories from the Old and New Testament, frescoes, paintings, "Pieta." In "Letter from the Drowned City (I)," she reveals something of the treasures submerged below the seas of her poetic imagination:

> What years will pass as ours, hours as years in my drowned city,
> An Atlantis of forgotten palazzos and orchards
> (Lemons and pears thrust up from the waves as if on the palm of
> Neptune).
> A Venezia of flooded kitchens and frescoes, wardrobes,
> Mirrors, pearls in red velvet boxes, submerged
> And silent. Swans scull overhead on the surface,
> My love, as it is in heaven.

She may not recover the Atlantis of her quest, a faith that has drowned, but she has elegantly saved snatches of a prayer, the echo of the Lord's Prayer. Her art allows her to swim for a safe passage, to stay afloat as it were, to seek salvage if not salvation. Heaven is still above her—a place where the living and the breathing aspire to rise.

Jennifer Atkinson teaches at George Mason University in Fairfax, VA. She is married to Eric Pankey; they have a daughter.

CONTRIBUTOR NOTES

William F. Bell is a retired newspaper editor and columnist who lives in Lenox, Massachusetts. His poems have appeared in *Poetry*, *The Formalist*, and *Troubadour*.

Alan Berecka grew up in Stittville, New York. He lives in Sinton, Texas, with his wife and two children. A product of the writing program at the University of North Texas, his publications include *The American Literary Review*, *The Windhover*, and *New Texas*. He earns his keep at Del Mar College in Corpus Christi where he is a reference librarian.

Deborah Bowen teaches in the English Department at Redeemer University College, a small Christian liberal arts university in S.W. Ontario. She has lived in Canada for 24 years, but still dreams of English country gardens.

Kathryn R. Campbell graduated from the Episcopal Seminary of the Southwest in Austin, Texas, with a Master of Arts in Pastoral Ministry. She is a Licensed Professional Counseling Intern at St. Peter-Joseph Children's Home in San Antonio working with both children and adults as an arts therapist, spiritual director and pastoral counselor. Her poems have previously been published in *The Journal of Pastoral Care*.

Donald Carlson lives in Fort Worth with his wife and four children. He is the middle school principal and teaches creative writing at Trinity Valley School in Fort Worth. Dr. Carlson is also a Fellow at the College of Saint Thomas More. His poetry has appeared in *Chronicles*, *Poem*, *Poetry Dallas*, and *The Pawn Review*.

Tony Clark writes poetry, fiction, and drama. A retired teacher of college English, he lives in Georgetown, Texas.

SuzAnne C. Cole, a former college English instructor, wrote *To Our Heart's Content: Meditations for Women Turning 50*. She's also published essays, poetry, plays, and short fiction in a wide range of commercial and literary publications.

Hugh Cook has published two books of short fiction, *Cracked Wheat and Other Stories* (1985); *Home In Alfalfa* (1998), and a novel, *The Homecoming Man* (1989) with Mosaic Press. He is Professor of English at Redeemer University College in Hamilton, Ontario. In 1997 the Evangelical Fellowship of Canada named him a recipient of the Leslie K. Tarr Award for his contribution to Christian writing.

Chet Corey is a Covenant Affiliate of the Franciscan Sisters of Perpetual Adoration (La Crosse, WI). His poetry has most recently appeared in the *National Catholic Reporter, A New Song, Re-Imagining*, and *St. Anthony Messenger*.

Jeffrey DeLotto, Professor of English at Texas Wesleyan University in Fort Worth, teaches writing, Shakespeare, Victorian literature, and modern British literature, when not working on his own poetry and prose.

Pennylyn Dykstra-Pruim taught three years at Brown University before joining the faculty of Calvin College as a research associate and a professor of German-English Applied Linguistics. Her current projects include *Auf geht's!*– a CDrom-based curriculum for introductory German, creative writing, and the more important tasks of assuring that her children bloom more beautifully than her garden, that her home is decorated with the faces of friendship and that her varied endeavors provide far more enjoyment than strain.

Jeffrey DeLotto, Professor of English at Texas Wesleyan University, teaches writing and British literature, when not working on his own poetry and prose. He has also taught writing and literature at Texas Tech University, Yarmouk University (Jordan), and the University of Plovdiv Fulbright Lecturer in American Literature in Bulgaria).

Myrna Downer is a writer who has a love of nature and God. She began writing poetry as a young girl and eventually began writing short stories and song lyrics. Her work has been published in *Whetstone, Vintage 96* (The League of Canadian Poets), *Esprit*, and *Winnipeg*. She had a lyrical story entitled *Paper Tears* broadcast twice on CBC Radio's *Alberta Anthology*.

Sharon Dunn publishes articles on writing, plays, skits and short stories when she is not chasing after her three children. She would like to dedicate this story to her mother, Mary Ellen, who died from breast cancer before she saw her grandchildren.

Chris Ellery teaches creative writing and American literature at Angelo State University. His poems and short stories have appeared in numerous journals, including the *Cloverdale Review, New Mexico Humanities Review, Suddenly*, and the *Christian Science Monitor*. A Fulbrighter in Syria from 1999-2000, he and his Syrian collaborator have recently completed a translation of *What Happened to Antara*, a volume of short stories by the award-winning Syrian playwright and novelist Walid Ikhlassi.

Ted Estess is a professor of English and Dean of The Honors College at the University of Houston. Author of a book on Elie Wiesel and of several articles on Samuel Beckett, he now writes principally on twentieth-century American authors. The present essay is taken from his manuscript of non-fiction entitled *Fishing Spirit Lake*, portions of which have previously appear in *Image* and *The Journal of the National Collegiate Honors Council*. A companion piece to the essay appeared in Windhover (Volume 5).

Greg Garrett is a past winner of the William Faulkner Prize for Fiction and author of the novel *Free Bird* (Kensington, 2002) and forty published short stories. He teaches at Baylor University, where he directs the anual Art & Soul conference, and lives in Austin, Texas, with his family.

Alan P. R. Gregory is the Frederic and Alma R. Duncalf Associate Professor of Church History at the Episcopal Seminary of the Southwest. Professor Gregory taught historical and systematic theology at Salisbury and Wells Theological College, England, before coming to the United States for doctoral studies at Emory University in the late 1980s. He earned his Ph.D. in historical theology, specializing in Romanticism and the work of Samuel Taylor Coleridge. Professor Gregory has complemented his teaching and research with service in numerous parochial ministries in Britain and Atlanta, Georgia.

Albert Haley is writer in residence at Abilene Christian University where he teaches fiction and poetry workshops. His poetry has most recently appeared in *Suddenly IV* and *Inside Grief: Death, Loss and Bereavement, an Anthology*.

H. Palmer Hall's fourth book is *Deep Thicket & Still Waters*. His work has recently appeared in *The North American Review, The Texas Review, The Briarcliff Review, Ascent,* and other literary magazines. He directs the library, teaches English and co-publishes Pecan Grove Press at St. Mary's University in San Antonio, Texas. This is his second appearance in *Windhover.*

Jerry Hamby teaches English and humanities at Lee College in Baytown. He has twice won creative writing awards from the Conference of College Teachers of English. His poetry has been published in *CCTE Studies, Concho River Review, Descant,* and *New Texas*. His fiction has appeared in the *Houston Chronicle* and Buffalo Press. In 2000, he participated in the West Texas A&M University Summer Writing Program.

Jeanette Hardage and her husband enjoy life in South Carolina, with a lovely swamp and an occasional alligator out back. A freelance writer and poet, she has also served three years as book review editor for *Christianity and the Arts*. She has work forthcoming in *Mars Hill Review and International Bulletin of Missionary Research.*

Anne Higgins is a member of the Daughters of Charity. She teaches and works in campus ministry at Mount Saint Mary's College in Emmitsburg, Maryland. Her poems have appeared in *Commonweal, Spriituality and Health, Yankee, College English,* and *The English Journal*. Her first book of poetry, *At the Year's Elbow*, was published by the Mellen Poetry Press in 2000.

Anne Hoffmann is the Minister of Congregational Life at the First Congregational Church of Shrewsbury, Massachusetts. She is a graduate of Union Theological Seminary in New York City, a member of Actor's Equity, and a percussionist. This is her first publication.

James Hoggard, a former NEA Fellow, is the author of fifteen books and the winner of awards in poetry, fiction, journalism, and literary translation. He is the Perkins-Prothro Distinguished Professor of English at Midwestern State University in Wichita Falls

Gail White's first full-length poetry collection, *The Price of Everything*, was published by Mellen Press in 2001. However, she still hasn't quit her day job as a medical transcriptionist. She lives in Breaux Bridge, Louisiana, with her husband, Arthur, and cats, Pushkin and Daisy.

Rhoda Janzen held the California Poet Laureate Award in 1994 and 1997; she publishes in journals like *The Yale Review* and *The Gettysburg Review* and recently appeared in the 2001 PBS television series *Closer To Truth.* Currently she teaches American Literature and Creative Writing at Hope College in Holland, Michigan.

Janet Kaderli is a wife, mother, writer, and musician. After teaching in public school for eighteen years, she is presently a full-time writer. The poem, "Joyful Noise" was written in Moab, Utah, and inspired by God's handiwork in Arches National Park.

Janet Kelley is a graduate of Saint Mary's College, South Bend, Indiana, and a recent graduate of the University of Notre Dame (MA in Theology). She currently works as an ESL instructor and also teaches adult education classes for the Fort Wayne/ South Bend Diocese in Indiana. Ms. Kelley would like to thank her poetry professor at Saint Mary's, Max Westler, for his encouragement.

Scott La Counte lives in California. This story was written when he was an undergraduate at Cal State Fullerton. He's currently in graduate school.

Nancy Tupper Ling from Walpole, Massachusetts is a poet/librarian/domestic Engineer...not usually in that order. Recent publication credits include *Flyway, Rambunctious Review, The Banner* and *The Aardvark Adventurer.*

Michael H. Lythgoe currently develops educational and cultural programs for the Smithsonian Associates. His photo of the iron cross sculpture in Purcellville, Virginia, by the late Frederick Hart, was on the cover of the last *Windhover*; his photo of Grace Episcopal Church in the Plains, Virginia is on the cover of the current issue. One of his poems was selected for publication in the 50th anniversary issue (poetry) of *Christianity and Literature*, spring 2001. His poem, "Good & Bad Tastes" won second prize in the Say the Word National Poetry Contest of Poems about Food. His poems, reviews and interviews have been published in *Windhover, The Writer's Chronicle, New Texas 99, South Dakota Review, Arcturus, The Caribbean Writer, Edge City Review, Christianity and Literature*, and elsewhere. He holds the MFA from Bennington College. Mike resides with his wife, Louise, in Gainesville, Virginia, near the Manassas National Battlefield Park.

Walt McDonald was an Air Force pilot, taught at the Air Force Academy, and served as Texas Poet Laureate for 2001. He has published nineteen collections of poetry and fiction, including *All Occasions* (Notre Dame, 2000), *Blessings the Body Gave* (Ohio State, 1998), and others from Harper & Row, Massachusetts, North Texas, and Pittsburgh. Four books have won Western Heritage Awards from the National Cowboy Hall of Fame.

John McKernan teaches at Marshall University in West Virginia. His *Postcard from Dublin* from recently published as a chapbook by Dead Metaphor Press in Boulder. Recent poems of his will soon appear in *The Paris Rveiew, West Branch, Heel Tap*, and *The Georgia Review*.

Leo Luke Marcello's poetry books include *Nothing Grows in One Place Forever, Silent Film, Blackrobe's Love Letters*, and *The Secret Proximity of Everywhere*. He is Professor of English in the Department of Languages at McNeese State University.

Lianne Mercer is a poet, fiction writer, and certified poetry therapist. Her short story, "The Game," was a finalist in the Judy and A.C. Greene Literary Festival of the Living Room Theatre of Salado, 2001. She is co-editor and publisher of the Texas Poetry Calendar.

Scott Moncrieff's poems has recent poems in *The Nebraska Review, Light, Controlled Burn*, and *Red Rock Review*. He teaches English at Andrews University in Berrien Springs, Michigan.

Stella Nesanovich is Professor of English at McNeese State University in Lake Charles, Louisiana. Her poetry has appeared previously in *Windhover* as well as in *America, Anglican Theological Review, Poet Lore, Xavier Review, Christianity and Literature*, and elsewhere. She is the author of *A Brightness That Made My Soul Tremble: Poems on the Life of Hildegard of Bingen* (Thibodaux, LA: Blue Heron Press, 1996). She was selected by the Louisiana State Arts Council as recipient of an Artist Fellowship for 1999-2000. The poems based on the life of Mechthild of Magdeburg are taken from her chapbook manuscript, *Dance, Oh Heart, Double Round: A Life of Mechthild of Magdeburg*.

Angela O'Donnell teaches English and American literature at Loyola College in Maryland. She is particularly interested in exploring the relationship between poetry and faith, both as a poet and as a reader and teacher of literature. Her poems have appeared in *The Lyric, Blue Collar Review, Potomac Review, Xavier Review, American Poets and Poetry,* and *Edge City Review.*

L. L. (Larry) Ollivier is the author of three published collections of poetry: *Albert Einstein in Las Vegas* (chapbook), *The Voice of All Things, Singing,* and *Holding Up the Universe* (forthcoming). He has, in his still young life, taught college English, worked as a bookseller, insurance courier, lumberyard clerk, forklift driver, and janitor, and trained for the Ministry. He lives in Reno with his wife and two children.

Susan Palwick is an Assistant Professor of English at the University of Nevada, Reno.

Arthur Powers is a convert to Christianity from agnosticism. He first moved to Brazil in 1969 and has lived most of his adult life there. From 1985 to 1992 he and his wife, with their two daughters, worked for the Franciscan Friars in the Amazon, doing pastoral work and organizing community groups and rural workers unions in an area of heavy land conflict. The Powers now live in Rio de Janeiro. Mr. Powers received a Fellowship in Fiction from the Massachusetts Artists Foundation (1984) and first and second prizes for short stories from the National Catholic Press Association (1995, 1998). In addition to *Windhover,* his poetry, fiction, and essays have appeared in *America, Americas Review, Commonweal, Hiram Poetry Review, Kansas Quarterly, New Blackfriars, Rattapallax, Roanoke Review, St. Anthony Messenger, Southern Poetry Review, Southwest Review, Texas Quarterly,* and many others.

Kathryn Thompson Presley, a retired English professor, has published numerous poems, short stories, and essays. She enjoys reading, speaking to women's groups and playing Scrabble with her grandchildren. She has been married almost fifty years to Roy Presley, a retired school administrator.

Cleatus Rattan ranches three miles south of Cisco, Texas, which is 103 miles west of Ft. Worth. His book, *The Border* is scheduled to reach print in the Fall from the *Texas Review Press.*

Mary Harwell Sayler has been a full-time writer for thirty years and poetry instructor for twenty – occasionally leading workshops and judging annual poetry competitions. Her many poems have appeared in religious and literary journals while her devotionals, books for children, and inspirational romances have been published by various Christian houses. Recently her correspondence course, *Poetry Writing, 1-On-1,* and *The Beginning Poet's Question & Answer Book,* became available electronically through RSVP Press with a "how-to" for poets through Dream Jobs To Go.

Brent Short lives in Atlanta, Georgia. He works at Mercer University as a reference librarian.

M. Bennet Smith studied poetry at George Fox University. His poetry and criticism have recently appeared in *Poem, Concho River Review*, and *Small Press Review*.

Virgil Suárez was born in Havana, Cuba. He is the author of four published novels: *Latin Jazz, The Cutter, Havana Thursdays*, and *Going Under*. With his wife Delia Poey he has co-edited two best-selling anthologies: *Iguana Dreams: New Latino Fiction* and *Little Havana Blues: A Contemporary Cuban-American Literature Anthology*. Most recently he has published an anthology of Latino poetry titled *Paper Dance* co-edited with Victor Hernández Cruz and Leroy V. Quintana, and his own collection of poetry and memoir titled *Spared Angola: Memories From a Cuban-American Childhood*. With Ryan G. Van Cleave he has edited *American Diaspora: Poetry of Displacement* and the forthcoming *Like Thunder: Poets Respond to Violence in America*. His work has been published in *TriQuarterly, Ontario Review, Parnassus, Cimarron, Meridian, Callaloo, Crazy Horse, The Caribbean Review, Salmagundi, New England Review, Ploughshares, The Mississippi Review, The Kenyon Review*, and *Prairie Schooner*.

Larry D. Thomas, a previous contributor of poetry to *Windhover*, lives and writes in Houston and Galveston, Texas. An Active Member of Western Writers of America, he has poems forthcoming in *Poet Lore, The Midwest Quarterly, The Chattahoochee Review, The Texas Review, Writers' Forum, American Indian Culture and Research Journal* and elsewhere. In September 2000, his manuscript *The Woodlanders* was selected as a finalist in the Summer 2000 Pecan Grove Press national chapbook competition, and will be published by the press in late 2001. His first collection of poems, *The Lighthouse Keeper*, was issued by Timberline Press in January 2001.

Carroll Yoder grew up on a farm in a close-knit Amish Mennonite community near Iowa City. He teaches French and English at Eastern Mennonite University in Harrisonburg, Virginia. Graduate study and five years of experience in Central Africa provided the impetus for his book, *White Shadows: A Dialectical View of the French African Novel*.

G. C. Waldrep had work recently in *Evansville Review* and *The Christian Century*. He has forthcoming in *Image, Gettysburg Review*, the special "spirituality" issue of *Many Mountains Moving*, and other journals. His recent residencies have been at Yaddo and MacDowell. His nonfiction book, *Southern Workers and the Search for Community*, was released in October 2000 by University of Illinois Press.

Leona Welch, of Denison, is an active member of the Poetry Society of Texas, National Federation of State Poetry Societies, A Galaxy of Verse Literary Foundation, and is serving her fifth year as Chair of Poetry in Schools of PST. Her award-winning poetry has been published in numerous anthologies and literary journals.

Gail White's first full-length poetry collection, *The Price of Everything*, was published by Mellen Press in 2001. However, she still hasn't quit her day job as a medical transcriptionist. She lives in Breaux Bridge, Louisiana, with her husband, Arthur, and cats, Pushkin and Daisy.

Leslie Williams received her Ph.D. from University of Houston and teaches English at Midland College. She has served a term as poetry editor of The Witness, and has published poetry in *New Texas, Cadence, Wild Cat, RiverSedge, Radix*, and a variety of other journals. She has published two books, *Seduction of the Lesser Gods* and *Night Wrestling*, which was a finalist for the Gold Medallion in 1997.

John Wolf holds a B.A. in Religious Studies from the University of Virginia and runs his own freelance writing business in the Chicago area. His poetry has appeared mostly in spiritual and interfaith journals, such as *Sufi* and *Sacred Journey*.

Robert Wooten has earned an MFA in poetry from the University of Alabama and earned an MA in creative writing from North Carolina State University. His poems have appeared in numerous periodicals and currently appear or are forthcoming in *Tucumcari Literary Review, Kimera, Old Red Kimono* and others. A limited edition of his chapbook, *Raymond Poems*, was published by Phoenix Press in 1999. He lives and works in Northport, Alabama.

Fredrick Zydek is the author of four collections of poetry: *Lights Along the Missouri, Storm Warning, Ending the Fast*, and *The Conception Abbey Poems*. His work appears in *The Antioch Review, Christianity Today, The Hollins Critic, Michigan Quarterly Review, Poetry, Poetry Northwest, Theology Today* and other journals. Formerly a professor of creative writing and theology at the University of Nebraska and later at the College of Saint Mary, he is now a gentleman farmer when he isn't writing. Most recently he has accepted the post as editor for Lone Willow Press.